Foreign Language Teaching in U.S. Schools

Results of a National Survey

Nancy C. Rhodes and Ingrid Pufahl

CAL

Foreign Language Teaching in U.S. Schools: Results of a National Survey

Published in the United States of America
Printed in Colombia by D´vinni S.A.

10 9 8 7 6 5 4 3 2 1

Editing: Jeanne Rennie and Julia Bozzolo
Proofreading: Amy Fitch
Cover and interior design: Santillana USA
Layout and production: Santillana USA

ISBN: 978-0-87281-006-8

Funding for the research that led to the development of this publication was provided by the following:

U.S. Department of Education
Office of Postsecondary Education
International Research and Studies Program
Grant No. P017A060006-08

The opinions expressed in this publication are those of the authors and do not necessarily reflect the positions or policies of any office of the U.S. Department of Education.

The design, layout, and printing of *Foreign Language Teaching in U.S. Schools: Results of a National Survey* were generously provided by Santillana USA.

To my father, who sparked my interest in languages.

NCR

To Ad, Nicolas, and Christina, who each have their own way of learning languages.

IP

TABLE OF CONTENTS

LIST OF TABLES AND FIGURES

Tables

Figures

ACKNOWLEDGMENTS

Many individuals and groups contributed to the success of the survey and to the publication of this report. We are especially grateful to the following individuals:

Marcia Rosenbusch (National K-12 Foreign Language Resource Center at Iowa State University), our project advisor, for providing advice and suggestions from the early proposal stage to the final report

Helena Curtain (University of Wisconsin, Milwaukee, retired), Dorry Kenyon (Center for Applied Linguistics), and Humphrey Tonkin (University of Hartford) for reviewing the draft report

Emma Muñoz (Language Matters) for assisting with the qualitative data analysis

Marty Abbott (American Council on the Teaching of Foreign Languages), Therese Caccavale (Holliston Public Schools, Massachusetts), and Mimi Met (National Foreign Language Center) for providing guidance in the data analysis

Brian Kleiner (formerly of Westat and currently at the Swiss Foundation for Research in Social Sciences in Lausanne) for working tirelessly with us from the conceptualization stage of this project and providing strong guidance on all aspects of sampling design and data analysis throughout the survey

We offer our sincere appreciation to the following staff members at Westat for their assistance throughout the project, especially with sampling procedures, survey design, data entry, and statistical analyses:

Debbie Alexander
Robert Delfierro
Libby Farris
Marian Harper
Randy Herbison
Kristin Madden
Anjali Pandit
Kimberley Raue
Manjula Thekdi

We are also indebted to the following groups for their support, suggestions, and feedback:

American Association of Teachers of French
American Association of Teachers of German
American Association of Teachers of Italian
American Association of Teachers of Spanish and Portuguese
American Classical League
American Council on the Teaching of Foreign Languages
Iowa State University National K-12 Foreign Language Resource Center
Joint National Committee for Languages
Modern Language Association
National Association of District Supervisors of Foreign Languages
National Council of Japanese Language Teachers
National Council of State Supervisors for Languages
National Network for Early Language Learning

Special thanks go to the following individuals who reviewed the draft questionnaires and provided useful suggestions:

Jayne Abrate
J. David Edwards
Eduardo Garcia
David Goldberg
David Jahner
Jean LeLoup
Eileen Lorenz
Zee Ann Poerio
Paul Sandrock
Martin Smith
Emily Spinelli
Helene Zimmer-Loew

We especially want to thank the teachers who pretested the questionnaires:

Opal Anderson-Curling
Nancy Barber
Jeannette Barretto
Emily Beeman
Deb Blaz
Elizabeth Caspari
Marissa Coulehan
Kathy DeBoer
Shanon de Joode
Danielle Deragisch
Brian Drost
Brandy Flack
Beverly Griffin
Fadia Hamid
Sandra Howard
Aviva Kadosh
Ray Kane
Ronnie Konner
Marina López
Lori Marusic
Kelli McCully
Sherri Nahum
Kathy Olson-Studler
Kelley Parkhurst
Candy Rice
Sierra Roussos
Nadine Salmon
Kathleen Siddons
Dawn Simonsen
Katherin Smith
Julie Stack
Sebastiano Stellato
Marianna Steriadis
Michelle Swope
Tricia Wu
Mary Young
Laura Zinke

Additionally, our gratitude goes to all the groups and individuals at the national, regional, state, and local levels who publicized the survey and helped us get a high response rate:

Michele Aoki (Washington)
Edward Bortot (New Mexico)
Karen Cardenas (South Dakota)
Kin Chee (New York)
Desa Dawson (Oklahoma)
Pamela Delfosse (Wisconsin)
Phyllis Farrar (Kansas)
Lynette Fujimori (Hawaii)
Greg Fulkerson (NADSFL)
Terri Hammatt (Louisiana)
Harry Haskell (Los Angeles)
Janice Kittok (Minnesota)
Pam Kollega (Pennsylvania)
Adriana Melnyk (Indiana)
Katherine López Natale (Massachusetts)
Paula Patrick (Virginia)
Cheri Quinlan (New Jersey)
Donald Reutershan (Maine)
Deborah Robinson (Ohio)
Lisa Saavedra (Florida)
Martie Semmer (Colorado)
Duarte Silva (California)
Susan C. Spinnato (Maryland)
Maria Trevino (Texas)

Many thanks also go to our colleagues at CAL who provided feedback and support for the project:

Donna Christian, CAL President, for providing guidance throughout the project

Huy Nguyen for designing the online survey and the database

Jacqueline López, Emma Muñoz, Chioma Chukwu, Marie Duré, Katie Kim, and Allison Wachter for contacting thousands of schools during data collection

Chengbin Yin for conducting additional data analysis

Susan Gilson and Ryan Atkins for assisting with survey production and design and dissemination of survey results

Jeanne Rennie and Julia Bozzolo for revising, editing, and overseeing final production of the publication

Amy Fitch for proofreading the final publication

Lupe Hernández-Silva for providing patient, competent, and cheerful assistance through all stages of the survey project

We gratefully acknowledge the funding for this research from the U.S. Department of Education, Office of Postsecondary Education, International Research and Studies Program. We offer special thanks to our project officers, Ed McDermott and Samuel Eisen, for their assistance and encouragement.

We are also most appreciative of Santillana Publishers for working with us to produce a brochure of preliminary survey findings in 2008 and for providing the design, layout, and printing of this report.

Finally, we are extremely grateful to all the school principals, foreign language chairpersons, and teachers who contributed to this important national survey by taking time from their busy schedules to complete and return the questionnaires. Of course, any errors or omissions that occur in the report are ours alone.

NCR and IP

EXECUTIVE SUMMARY

In 2008, in collaboration with Westat, a statistical survey research organization, and with funding from the U.S. Department of Education's International Research and Studies Program, the Center for Applied Linguistics (CAL) conducted a nationwide survey of elementary and secondary schools to collect detailed information on foreign language education in the United States. The goal of the survey was to identify current patterns and shifts over time in five key areas: amount of foreign language instruction in schools, languages and types of programs offered, foreign language curriculum, teacher certification and professional development, and effects of education reform on language instruction. During the 2007–2008 school year, principals, foreign language teachers, and department chairs from a nationally representative sample of more than 5,000 public and private schools completed CAL's four-page survey.

The 2008 survey results complement and enhance the field's existing knowledge base regarding foreign language instruction and enrollment in the United States. The full report of the survey offers comparisons of the 2008 data with data collected by CAL in its two previous national surveys, conducted in 1987 and 1997. This summary presents highlights of the survey results.

Amount of Language Instruction

The percentage of elementary and middle schools offering foreign language instruction decreased significantly from 1997 to 2008: from 31% to 25% of all elementary schools (Figure 1) and from 75% to 58% of all middle schools. The decline at the elementary level occurred mainly in public elementary schools; the percentage of private elementary schools teaching languages remained about the same. The percentage of high schools teaching foreign languages stayed relatively steady at about 91% (Figure 2). Only a small percentage of the schools not teaching languages in 2008 expressed an interest in offering languages in the next 2 years: 8% of elementary schools and 17% of secondary schools (Figures 3 and 4).

Survey results revealed issues of unequal access to foreign language instruction. Schools in rural areas and schools whose students were of lower socioeconomic status (SES) were less likely to offer foreign language classes. In addition, the percentage of private elementary schools offering foreign language instruction (51%) was more than three times that of public elementary schools (15%).

Languages, Program Types, and Scheduling

The teaching of Spanish, the most commonly taught language, increased significantly at the elementary level (from 79% of schools with language programs in 1997 to 88% in 2008) and remained stable (93%) at the secondary level (Figures 5 and 6). The teaching of French and German, however, saw significant declines at both levels. French decreased from 27% to 11% of schools with language programs at the elementary level and from 64% to 46% at the secondary level. German decreased from 5% to 2% at the elementary level and from 24% to 14% at the secondary level.

The percentage of schools offering Chinese and Arabic, although still low, increased at both the elementary and secondary levels. In 2008, Chinese was taught at 3% of elementary schools and 4% of secondary schools with language programs. The percentages for Arabic were 1% for elementary schools and 0.6% for secondary schools. Latin was down at the secondary level (from 20% to 13%) but rose at the elementary level (from 3% to 6%). The teaching of Russian and Japanese decreased at both levels.

Among public elementary schools, the most commonly offered foreign language program was the exploratory model (offered by 47% of public elementary schools with language programs), which provides introductory exposure to the language. Language focus programs, which emphasize listening, speaking, reading, writing, and culture, were offered at 39% of public elementary schools with language programs

(Table 21 and Figure 8). These programs may or may not expect students to gain proficiency in the language, depending on the goals of the particular program. The remaining 14% of programs followed an immersion model, which provides students the opportunity to attain high levels of proficiency in the target language.

Most secondary schools with language programs (95%) offered standard classes with instruction in listening, speaking, reading, writing, and culture (Figure 9). The percentage of secondary schools offering Advanced Placement (AP) language classes increased significantly: from 12% in 1987 to 16% in 1997 to 21% in 2008.

Curriculum and Instruction

As was true in past surveys, the vast majority of secondary school language programs reported having an established foreign language curriculum. At the elementary school level, the percentage of elementary school language programs with an established curriculum increased gradually over 20 years, from 64% in 1987 to 78% in 2008.

The use of literature from the target culture increased significantly at both the elementary and secondary levels from 1997 to 2008. There was also a noticeable increase in the use of technology-based instructional materials. The use of Internet resources tripled at the elementary level and doubled at the secondary level, and the use of computer-assisted instructional materials and other instructional technology (e.g., satellite broadcasts, interactive television, video conferencing) increased significantly at both levels (Tables 32 and 33).

Survey results revealed an increase by both elementary and secondary schools in the use of proficiency-oriented assessments, including oral presentations, oral interviews, and student portfolios. There was also an increase at both levels in the use of student self-assessments, in which students take an active role in monitoring their language development.

Teachers in 2008 reported using the foreign language in the classroom more than they did in 1997. About one third of elementary and secondary schools with language programs reported that their teachers used the target language in class at least 75% of the time. In 1997, the percentage for secondary school teachers was only 22% (Figures 19 and 20). (Elementary schools were not asked the question in 1997.)

Only 39% of elementary schools with language programs reported some type of articulation from elementary to middle school foreign language instruction (Figure 22). A higher percentage of high schools—55% of those whose students had studied a language in middle school—reported having an articulated sequence of instruction from middle school to high school (Figure 23). This was a notable increase from 24% in 1997.

At both the elementary and secondary levels, the percentage of schools whose language teachers incorporated national or state standards into their instruction almost tripled from 1997 to 2008.

Foreign Language Teachers

More than one quarter of all elementary school foreign language teachers are not certified at all. The percentage of elementary schools that reported having uncertified language teachers increased from 17% in 1997 to 31% in 2008. At the same time, the percentage of schools that reported having at least one teacher with K–12 foreign language teacher certification increased from 19% to 34%, and the percentage reporting at least one teacher with elementary foreign language teacher certification increased from 19% to 24%. At the secondary school level, the overwhelming majority of schools reported that their language teachers were certified, with 77% holding a secondary level foreign language teaching certificate and 44% holding a K–12 foreign language teaching certificate. (Some teachers held more than one type of certificate.)

Although most schools at both levels reported that their teachers had engaged in subject-specific professional development within the previous year (63% elementary, 73% secondary), the level of participation at both levels was unchanged from 1997 to 2008. There was a significant disparity between rural schools and urban and suburban schools. Teachers in rural schools had a much lower rate of participation in professional development.

One quarter (25%) of elementary schools and nearly one third (30%) of secondary schools offering languages reported being affected by a shortage of qualified language teachers. The schools most affected were elementary schools in rural areas and elementary and secondary schools with a large percentage of students from low socioeconomic backgrounds (Figure 30).

Educational Reform

At both the elementary and secondary levels, the percentage of schools whose language teachers incorporated national or state standards into their instruction almost tripled from 1997 to 2008. Standards use increased from 25% to 76% in public elementary schools and from 31% to 89% in public secondary schools (Figures 31 and 32).

Approximately one third of public elementary and secondary schools with language programs reported that their foreign language instruction had been affected by the federal No Child Left Behind (NCLB) education legislation (Figure 33). Comments from survey respondents suggested that NCLB's focus on mathematics and reading instruction had drawn resources away from foreign languages because they are not included in the law's accountability measures.

Conclusion

The profile of foreign language instruction in the United States revealed by the 2008 survey shows that foreign language instruction remained relatively stable at the high school level from 1997 to 2008 but that it decreased substantially in elementary and middle schools. Moreover, only a small percentage of the elementary and middle schools not teaching languages in 2008 planned to implement a language program within the next 2 years.

Survey data revealed a number of other disturbing trends:

- There were inequities in access to foreign language education. Languages were offered in smaller percentages of rural schools and low SES schools whose students were from lower socioeconomic backgrounds.
- The teaching of French, German, Japanese, and Russian decreased at both the elementary and secondary levels.
- Nearly one third of public elementary and secondary schools with language programs reported that language teaching had been negatively affected by NCLB.
- The disparity between public and private elementary school language offerings increased exponentially, with private schools offering languages at much higher rates.

- The shortage of language teachers was so severe that some schools were seeking alternative sources of teachers, such as agencies that provide teachers from other countries, commercial language schools, and foreign governments that send teachers to the United States.

Some positive trends are also evident from the survey results:

- The teaching of Arabic and Chinese increased at both the elementary and secondary levels.
- Language teachers at both the elementary and secondary levels were integrating national and state language standards into their teaching more than they did a decade earlier and using the target language in the classroom more frequently.
- There were pockets of innovation—in particular, immersion programs where elementary schools offered language instruction resulting in high levels of proficiency.
- More language classes were using authentic literature from the target culture than before.
- The use of technology-based materials—Internet resources, computer-assisted instructional materials, instructional technology—increased significantly.
- Both elementary and secondary schools continued to offer language classes for native speakers—mostly in Spanish, but in some other languages as well.

Unfortunately, the overall picture of foreign language instruction in 2008 was no better—and in some areas worse—than in 1997. There continues to be reason for serious concern about the limited number of long-sequence K–12 language programs designed to provide students with the linguistic and cultural skills needed to communicate effectively in the United States and abroad. In addition, the gap has widened between the haves and the have-nots. A large number of elementary and middle school students in this country, especially those in rural or low SES schools, do not have the opportunity to study foreign language at all.

It is time for all Americans to recognize the vital importance of an American citizenry that can communicate effectively in many languages and across cultures, and for schools to make the teaching and learning of foreign languages a priority in the K–12 curriculum. When legislators, administrators, and other education policy makers recognize the need to incorporate foreign languages into the core curriculum, the necessary funding and other resources will follow. This change in attitude is the necessary first step in moving our country toward parity with nations around the globe that graduate students who can communicate in more than one language.

PART 1
Introduction

CHAPTER 1: INTRODUCTION

In the increasingly interconnected world of the 21st century, Americans need to be able to communicate in more than one language. U.S. policy makers, educators, parents, business leaders, and major research organizations are calling for an education system that prepares students to become competent world citizens who can communicate effectively in English and other languages (Partnership for 21st Century Skills, 2007). Although English has become a global *lingua franca,* many believe that the world standard for global communication "is not English, but rather bilingualism and cross-cultural communication" (Grandin, 2006, p. 184), because "the only real way to interact with persons from other cultures is through their own view of the world, and that means their language" (Grandin, 2001).

The call for more and better foreign language[1] instruction is nothing new. For decades, policymakers, business leaders, high-level commissions, educators, and members of the public have recognized that the United States needs to increase the number of individuals in this country who can communicate in languages other than English (Jackson & Malone, 2009). Federal education legislation enacted in 1994 (Goals 2000: Educate America Act, 1994) postulated that "by the year 2000, all American students will leave Grades 4, 8, and 12 having demonstrated competency over challenging subject matter including English, mathematics, science, foreign language and the percentage of all students who are competent in more than one language will substantially increase."

Since that time, increased economic globalization and international terrorism have added urgency to the need for Americans who can interact effectively with people from other cultures. In 2004, the U.S. Department of Defense and the Center for Advanced Study of Language sponsored the National Language Conference—a gathering of language and policy experts from all levels of government, all levels of education, heritage language communities, and the private sector. The outcome of this conference was *A Call to Action for National Foreign Language Capabilities* (2005), a white paper calling for action on the foreign language and cultural capabilities of the nation in three areas (p. 2):

- National security: Gathering and analyzing information, advancing international diplomacy, sustaining military operations, and protecting the U.S. homeland
- Economic competitiveness: Retaining leadership in the global marketplace, entering local markets, competing with increasingly sophisticated international competitors whose "workforces possess potent combinations of professional skills, knowledge of other cultures, and multiple language proficiencies"
- Domestic well-being: Providing opportunities for all students to learn foreign languages important for the nation, developing the capabilities of heritage communities, and ensuring equal access to services that are core to American quality of life

[1] The phrase *foreign language* is used in this report to refer to any language other than English. We recognize, however, that the use of the word *foreign* to describe languages other than English is becoming increasingly problematic in the U.S. context (National Standards in Foreign Language Education Project, 2006, p.27). Many of the languages taught in U.S. schools are not foreign to all students (e.g., Chinese, Spanish, Vietnamese), and many are not foreign to the United States (e.g., Native American Languages, American Sign Language). Many states and school districts have recognized this and are now using terms such as *world languages, second languages,* or *languages other than English.* For this report, however, we decided to use the term *foreign language* because we believed it would be the most widely recognized and understood.

Based on the consensus that the "demand for individuals with foreign language skills and cultural understanding far outweighs the supply" (p. 5), the National Language Conference recommended provisions to increase and improve long-sequence K–16 foreign language education, teacher training, teaching practices, standardized assessment, and instructional materials and technological tools, particularly in languages deemed critical to the nation, such as Arabic, Chinese, Farsi, and Russian.

The need for increased foreign language instruction was in the spotlight again in 2006, when the President proposed the National Security Language Initiative to increase funding for early foreign language education, teacher training, and immersion and study abroad programs in critical languages (U.S. Department of Education, 2006). That same year, the Committee for Economic Development (2006), an organization of more than 200 business leaders and university presidents, issued a report reiterating the warning that the United States will lose its leadership role in the global economy unless its education system can address the dearth of Americans who are fluent in foreign languages, particularly critical and less commonly taught languages. Addressing a narrowing of the curriculum as a result of the focus on mathematics and reading in the federal No Child Left Behind (NCLB) education legislation, the report warned of the elimination or reduction of foreign language programs, especially as other countries increasingly emphasize the international education of their students from an early age (Education, Audiovisual and Culture Executive Agency, 2008).

International studies show that both U.S.-based multinational companies and small businesses need employees with foreign language and culture skills to market their products to customers around the world and to work with their employees and business partners abroad (Committee for Economic Development, 2006, 6ff.). In fact, in a 2002 survey of large U.S. companies (Kedia & Daniel, as cited in Committee for Economic Development, 2006), nearly 30% reported having lost business abroad because their employees lacked the necessary language and culture skills. Recommendations from the Committee for Economic Development to sustain global economic leadership included teaching international content across the curriculum at all levels of education and creating a pipeline of foreign language learners that starts in elementary school and continues through postsecondary education. Specifically, schools should "implement language programs in the elementary grades and offer more advanced language classes in middle schools and high schools" (Committee for Economic Development, 2006, p. 27).

Tracking the Status of U.S. Foreign Language Education

How can we gauge the country's progress in educating students to become global citizens? How can we identify changes that may be needed to language education policies, instructional methods, and teacher preparation? Over the past two decades, the Center for Applied Linguistics (CAL) has gathered and analyzed data on foreign language instruction across the nation in order to provide a portrait of K–12 foreign language education in the United States and identify issues that need to be addressed. In 1987, with funding from the U.S. Department of Education, CAL conducted its first large-scale, nationwide survey of public and private elementary and secondary schools in the United States (Rhodes & Oxford, 1988). The survey included questions about the specific languages and types of programs offered, curricula, teacher qualifications and training, and student enrollment. CAL replicated its study in

International studies show that both U.S.-based multinational companies and small businesses need employees with foreign language and culture skills.

1997, providing the opportunity to examine changes in U.S. foreign language education over a 10-year period.

The 1997 survey results revealed that the availability of foreign language instruction in elementary schools had increased by nearly 10 percentage points nationwide (from 22% to 31% of all elementary schools) since 1987 and had stayed relatively stable at the secondary level. At both levels, more than half of the schools not teaching languages expressed an interest in doing so in the future. A number of other positive trends were evident from the 1997 survey results:

- An increase in the availability of language classes for native speakers (e.g., Spanish for Spanish speakers) at both elementary and secondary levels
- An increase in the teaching of Japanese at the elementary school level and Japanese and Russian at the secondary school level
- A significant increase in the use of computer-based instructional materials
- A significant increase in staff development and inservice training at both the elementary and secondary school levels
- An awareness of national or state standards for language learning among half the schools teaching languages

Despite these positive trends, the survey researchers expressed serious concern about the "limited number of K–12 long-sequence language programs designed to educate students linguistically and culturally to communicate successfully in the United States and abroad." They concluded that "well-articulated elementary and secondary programs are still the exception rather than the rule, and intensive instruction that aims at a high level of proficiency, as outlined in the national standards, is scarce" (Rhodes & Branaman, 1999, p.71).

In 2008, CAL again conducted a nationwide survey of foreign language instruction in U.S. elementary and secondary schools. Like its 1987 and 1997 predecessors, the 2008 survey was designed to provide both national and regional profiles of foreign language instruction in the United States. The survey results can be used to determine the extent and effectiveness of foreign language instruction across the country and to assess how well the United States is preparing students to meet the acute need for individuals who can communicate in languages other than English. The results of CAL's 2008 survey are the subject of this book.

The 2008 Survey

The 2008 survey of public and private elementary and secondary schools was conducted in collaboration with Westat, a statistical survey research organization, under a grant from the U.S. Department of Education, International Research and Studies Program. As with the previous surveys, CAL's goal was to identify current patterns and shifts over time in foreign language enrollment, languages offered, models of instruction, curricula and methodologies, and teacher qualifications and training. The 2008 survey also included new questions about language teacher shortages, alternative means of hiring teachers, and the effects of the NCLB education legislation on foreign language programs. Principals, foreign language teachers, and department chairs from a nationally representative sample of more than 5,000 public and private schools completed a four-page questionnaire during the 2007-2008 school year.

Survey questions fell within five key topic areas: amount of foreign language instruction, languages and types of programs offered, foreign language curriculum, teacher qualifications and training, and educational reform issues. Questions marked with an asterisk (*) below were new for the 2008 survey; all other questions remained unchanged from the 1997 survey or had only minor changes. For example, the 1997 question "Does your school teach foreign language(s)?" was changed to "Does your school currently teach foreign language(s)?" to emphasize that we wanted data on the current year. (See Appendixes A and B for the actual elementary and secondary questionnaires.) The following is a summary of the survey questions:

- Amount of foreign language instruction
  - Does the school offer foreign language instruction?
  - If not, is it planning to start a program in the next 2 years?
  - How many students are enrolled in foreign language classes (by language)?

- Language and types of programs offered
  - What languages are taught?
  - What types of programs are most common?
  - What levels are offered for each language and how many minutes or hours per week do the classes meet?
  - When during the day are the classes taught? (elementary schools only)
  - When are the classes scheduled during the school year?

- Foreign language curriculum
  - Is there an established foreign language curriculum?
  - What types of instructional materials are used?
  - How is students' language proficiency assessed?
  - How much do the teachers use the foreign language in the classroom?* (new for elementary schools in 2008; asked only of secondary schools in 1997)
  - What type of sequencing, if any, is planned for the continuation of language study from elementary through secondary school?

- Teacher qualifications and training
  - How many teachers are there in each school?
  - What types of certification do the teachers have?
  - Did teachers participate in inservice training or professional development last year?
  - Is the school affected by the national teacher shortage?*
  - Are any language teachers hired through alternative means?* (asked of elementary schools only)

- Educational reform
  - Do the teachers integrate national and/or state foreign language standards into their instruction?
  - How has the foreign language program been affected by NCLB?*

Related Surveys

The results of CAL's survey are intended to be used in tandem with other available data on foreign language teaching. Although there is no systematic, centralized plan at the federal level for gathering foreign language data of this type, various organizations have compiled information that can be used to track foreign language enrollments and instruction. Two noteworthy surveys are the state survey conducted by the American Council on the Teaching of Foreign Languages (ACTFL) and the higher education survey conducted by the Modern Language Association (MLA).

ACTFL regularly surveys states to gather data on foreign language enrollment in public schools. Their most recent survey project, funded by the U.S. Department of Education, collected data by language and level of study and included detailed case studies

Principals, foreign language teachers, and department chairs from a nationally representative sample of more than 5,000 public and private schools completed a four-page questionnaire during the 2007–2008 school year.

from selected states (American Council on the Teaching of Foreign Languages, 2007). Their data sources included state departments of education, local education agencies, language-specific professional organizations, state language associations, and textbook publishers. ACTFL and CAL collaborated on their most recent surveys, consulting with each other on data-gathering methodologies and results.

The MLA regularly surveys U.S. institutions of higher education regarding their foreign language enrollments. The most recent MLA survey, conducted in 2006 with funding from the U.S. Department of Education, surveyed 2,801 colleges and universities (Furman, Goldberg, & Lusin, 2007). CAL follows MLA's higher education survey results to explore commonalities, differences, and articulation potential from elementary to secondary to college language instruction.

About This Report

This report includes highlights of the survey findings (see Executive Summary), a description of the survey methodology, presentation and discussion of survey results by topic, and recommendations for future action. It is hoped that the data reported here will guide efforts to increase and improve foreign language instruction in our schools. Educators will be able to see how their foreign language programs compare to those in a national sample. State departments of education and local school districts can use the data to inform the discussion, planning, and implementation of measures to improve foreign language teaching in their schools. Survey results can also be used by policy makers at the local, state, and national levels to inform decisions on language and education policy.

Lastly, this report provides the U.S. Department of Education with access to national data on foreign language education with two prior comparison points, allowing them to examine the impact of their programs in this area and plan for the future. CAL plans to continue conducting this survey every decade to track our nation's progress in providing opportunities for students to develop proficiency in other languages along with the skills to communicate effectively across cultures.

PART 2
Methodology

CHAPTER 2: METHODOLOGY

This chapter provides an overview of the methods used in the survey, including questionnaire development, sampling and weighting procedures, and data collection and analysis. A demographic profile of the schools that participated in the survey is also provided.

Questionnaire Development

Two separate but similar questionnaires were developed for elementary and secondary schools, with variations in item wording to reflect the two different levels of instruction (see Appendixes A and B). Whenever possible, individual survey items were worded identically to items in the 1997 survey to enhance the likelihood of comparable results.[2] Some items were changed, however, in order to collect more accurate and meaningful data reflecting changes in the profession. Two new questions were added to both questionnaires: one about teacher shortages and one about the effects of the No Child Left Behind Act on language instruction. Two additional questions were added to the elementary school questionnaire: one about hiring teachers through alternative means and one about teacher use of the target language. (The latter has always appeared on the secondary school questionnaire.) Two questions from the 1997 survey that did not result in useful responses were deleted.

These changes were based on suggestions from the senior project advisor, foreign language specialists, survey research consultants, and representatives of 13 key language organizations who reviewed drafts of the questionnaires: the American Associations of Teachers of French, German, Italian, and Spanish and Portuguese; the American Classical League; the American Council on the Teaching of Foreign Languages; Iowa State University National K–12 Foreign Language Resource Center; the Joint National Committee for Languages; the Modern Language Association; the National Association of District Supervisors of Foreign Languages; the National Council of Japanese Language Teachers; the National Council of State Supervisors for Languages; and the National Network for Early Language Learning.

Content validity of the survey items was assured through several survey reviews, including a formal clinical trial involving elementary and secondary principals and foreign language teachers. These pretests of the questionnaires ensured the clarity, appropriateness, and utility of each item. CAL staff pretested a print version of the elementary and secondary questionnaires with teachers and principals who were recruited via two email discussion groups for foreign language educators: FLTeach and Ñandu. Fifteen principals and foreign language teachers at each of the two levels completed surveys for their respective schools. CAL staff conducted follow-up interviews with each respondent to collect detailed information about their interpretation of the questions and about any questions they didn't understand, and solicited their comments on the survey procedure. In addition, 10 teachers and other language professionals pretested only the new survey questions and provided feedback. After reviewing all the questionnaire answers and respondents' comments, CAL staff revised the questionnaires accordingly.

CAL wanted to make the survey available only online, but survey design experts recommended that, for data comparability purposes with past surveys, the 2008 survey also be made available in print, as it was

[2] The survey data for the three time periods were collected during the school years of 1986–1987, 1996–1997, and 2007–2008, and are referred to as the 1987, 1997, and 2008 surveys. When relevant for a particular question, the data from all three time periods are presented.

in 1987 and 1997. So both print and online versions were developed. The layout of the online version was designed to reflect as much as possible the layout of the print version.

The online survey was tested on a variety of Internet browsers and by several survey experts for robustness of the system. Subsequently, CAL staff pretested the online questionnaire with 25 foreign language teachers and principals, eliciting detailed feedback on the user interface, ease of navigation, and clarity of page layout. Changes were made based on the feedback received to ensure content validity and the clarity, appropriateness, and utility of each item.

The survey instruments themselves were professionally designed for ease of response, with wide margins, easy-to-read type, and space for computer coding. The design and layout of the print survey was completed in collaboration with design specialists at EEI Communications, a publications company, which provided the final version using InDesign software. The online version was designed by in-house designers at CAL using the print survey as the template. As in the previous surveys, most of the items were close-ended questions with pre-coded response options, although space was provided for open-ended comments on some items.

Sampling and Weighting Procedures

Respondent Selection

The schools in the sample were selected through a stratified random sample design from universe lists (i.e., sampling frames) of public and private elementary and secondary schools in the United States. The sampling frame for public schools was the 2005–2006 Common Core of Data Public School Universe Survey File compiled and maintained by the National Center for Education Statistics. The sampling frame for private schools was the 2005–2006 Private School Survey Data File, also maintained by the National Center for Education Statistics. The public school frame contained a total of 85,719 schools, including 52,076 elementary schools, 31,804 secondary schools, and 1,839 schools with combined elementary and secondary grades. The private school frame represented a total of 27,389 schools, including 17,616 elementary schools, 2,921 secondary schools, and 6,852 schools with combined elementary and secondary grades. Because schools with combined elementary and secondary grades could respond to either the elementary or secondary school survey, they were placed in a separate stratum and given independent chances of selection for either the elementary or secondary survey (see Sample Stratification).

The elementary survey was sent to a sample of 3,561 schools, including 2,165 public elementary schools and 60 public combined (elementary and secondary) schools, for a total sample of 2,225 public schools; and to 927 private elementary schools and 409 private combined schools, for a total of 1,336 private schools. The secondary survey was sent to a sample of 1,554 schools, including 748 public secondary schools and 29 public combined schools, for a total sample of 777 public schools; and to 316 private secondary schools and 461 private combined schools, for a total sample of 777 private schools.

Sample Stratification[3]

The selection of schools for the 2008 survey was done within four major subgroups of schools, defined by crossing instructional level (elementary vs. secondary) with type of control (public vs. private). Both the elementary and secondary school frames included schools with combined elementary and secondary grades (the "combined" schools) because such schools could respond to either the elementary or secondary version of the survey. For public elementary schools, 10 sampling strata were defined by crossing level

[3] The specific labels used to describe the variables (e.g., small schools, very large schools; high SES, low SES; high minority enrollment, very high minority enrollment) were created for reporting purposes only, to make the text more readable. The authors are not suggesting, for example, that all schools in the nation with fewer than 400 students would be considered small schools outside the context of this report, or that all schools with a minority enrollment over 30% would be considered to have a high minority enrollment. The authors recognize that what constitutes high or low, small or large in a particular category may vary according to the local context.

(elementary vs. combined) with school size based on enrollment[4]:

<300 students
300–499 students
500–599 students
600–749 students
≥750 students

Within these strata, additional implicit stratification was induced by sorting the schools in the sampling frame by one or more of the following variables:

Metro status (city, urban fringe, town, rural)[5]

Geographic region[6] (Northeast, South, Southwest, Central, Pacific Northwest), as defined by the boundaries of the five regional foreign language conferences

Socioeconomic status (SES) as measured by the percentage of students eligible for free or reduced-price lunch

<20% eligible = high SES school
20%–39% eligible = medium SES school
40%–69% eligible = low SES school
≥70% eligible = very low SES school

Minority enrollment as measured by the percentage of students whose race or ethnicity is classified as American Indian or Alaska Native, Asian or Pacific Islander, non-Hispanic Black, or Hispanic

<10% = low minority enrollment
10%–29% = medium minority enrollment
30%–49% = high minority enrollment
≥50% = very high minority enrollment

A similar stratification was used for public secondary schools, but the sorting by school size was done according to the following ranges of enrollment figures[7]:

<300 students
300–499 students
500–999 students
1,000–1,499 students
≥1,500 students

For the private schools (both elementary and secondary), 10 sampling strata were defined by crossing level (elementary or secondary vs. combined) with school size based on enrollment. Within the private school strata, additional implicit stratification was induced by sorting the schools in the sampling frame by metro status, minority enrollment, and geographic region. Data on socioeconomic status were not available for private schools.

Prior to sampling, schools within a stratum were sorted by the variables indicated in the preceding paragraph. Using a random start, a systematic sample of schools was selected from each stratum at the rate specified for the stratum. The method of selection was essentially the same for each of the four major subgroups described above. For each level (elementary vs. secondary)/type-of-control (public vs. private) subgroup, within-stratum sampling rates were determined for the 10 sampling strata using the square-root method (i.e., the sample is allocated in proportion to the square root of the stratum population size). Thus, the total sample was allocated to the strata in rough proportion to the aggregate of the square root of

[4] For reporting purposes, these five categories were collapsed into four and labeled as follows:

<400 students = small schools
400–699 students = medium schools
700–999 students = large schools
≥1,000 students = very large schools

[5] For reporting purposes, the urban fringe and town categories were collapsed into a single category, called suburban.

[6] The regional results were compiled according to foreign language conference regions in order to assist the profession in planning regional initiatives. See Appendix C for the list of the states in each region.

[7] For reporting purposes, these five categories were collapsed into four, as follows:

<400 students = small schools
400–999 students = medium schools
1,000–1,399 students = large schools
≥1,400 students = very large schools

Table 1. Unweighted and Weighted Counts of Sample Schools[a]

	Public		Private	
	Elementary	Secondary	Elementary	Secondary
Schools selected for sample	2,225	777	1,336	777
Schools responding to the survey	1,835	519	833	483
Weighted count of schools responding to the survey	52,909	32,797	21,256	8,426
Schools offering foreign language completing the 2008 survey	257	426	481	452
Weighted count of schools offering foreign language completing the 2008 survey	7,800	25,057	10,887	7,434

[a] Categories are those specified for sampling and include combined schools.

the enrollment of the schools in the stratum. Such an allocation was expected to provide acceptable sampling precision for estimates of proportions as well as numeric measures correlated with the size of school.

Weighting for National Estimates

In general, weights are required for analysis of data from a stratified sample design. For the 2008 survey, the role of the sampling weights was to reflect the variable probabilities of selection with which schools were selected for the study and compensate for differential rates of nonresponse. Under the stratified sampling procedures described in the previous section, large schools were generally sampled at higher rates than smaller ones and thus should have correspondingly smaller weights than the small schools. Similarly, to compensate for survey nonresponse, schools with low response rates should have relatively larger nonresponse adjustments than schools with high response rates. Thus, the weight assigned to a particular responding school in the sample was computed from the general formula:

$$W = A_1A_2/f,$$

where f is the probability of selecting the school (i.e., the sampling rate), A_1 is an initial adjustment for nonresponding schools for which the presence of foreign language instruction was not ascertained, and A_2 is an adjustment for schools known to have foreign language instruction based on their responses to that specific question but that did not complete the survey. The first adjustment, A_1, was computed within homogeneous groups defined by stratum, setting, and region; the second adjustment, A_2, was computed within classes defined by stratum and type of language courses offered. Table 1 summarizes the final weighted counts of schools in the sample using the weights, W, computed from the above formula.

Table 2. Design Effect Weightings (DEFT)

YEAR	Type of estimate	Elementary sample	Secondary sample
1987	Overall	1.45	1.27
	Public	1.32	1.24
	Private	1.40	1.22
1997	Overall	1.53	1.32
2008	Overall	1.19	1.22
	Public	1.13	1.09
	Private	1.26	1.21

Adjustment of Simple Random Sample Standard Errors

As in the 1987 and 1997 surveys, the 2008 sample design used weights to adjust for disproportionate sampling of schools of various sizes (see Weighting for National Estimates). The weights are a component of the variability of the sample-based estimates. The square root of the design effect, or DEFT, is the effect on standard errors due to unequal weighting resulting from disproportionate sampling and differential nonresponse adjustments. Estimates of the DEFTs for the 2008 survey are provided in Table 2. The DEFTs were separated by level (elementary vs. secondary) and type of control (public vs. private) because the 2008 school samples were selected independently from each of these subgroups. The DEFTs for 1987 and 1997 are provided for reference and comparison (although private vs. public comparisons are not available for 1997). The standard error is computed as the standard error under a simple random sample multiplied by its DEFT. For example, if the simple random sample standard error for a given response from public elementary schools in the 2008 survey is 1%, the adjusted standard error is (1%)(1.13) = 1.13%.

Limitations of National Estimates

As is the case in virtually every sample survey, estimates derived from the 2008 foreign language survey are subject to limitations. Because the results are based on a sample, they are subject to sampling error. The calculated standard errors of the sample-based estimates can be used to construct confidence intervals that provide a measure of the margin of error of the estimate. In addition to sampling error, the estimates are subject to nonsampling error resulting from nonresponse, incorrect reporting of the survey data, keying errors, undercoverage of the sampling frame, and other sources. Confidence intervals computed from the survey data generally do not reflect the errors due to nonsampling sources. Nonsampling errors are minimized by employing strict quality control procedures in data processing and maintaining as high a response rate as possible through extensive follow-up. Nonresponse weighting adjustments of the types used to weight the survey data were designed to attenuate potential nonresponse biases.

Data Collection Procedures

The K-12 foreign language survey was conducted from October 2007 to June 2008, a time frame that parallels that of the two previous surveys, conducted during the 1986-1987 and 1996-1997 school years. In contrast to the 1987 and 1997 surveys, for which data were collected only by mail, the 2008 survey gave respondents the option of responding online via the Web or completing a print copy of the survey and returning it by mail or fax. Printed questionnaires, which also included information about how to complete the survey online, were prepared for the sample of 3,561 elementary schools and 1,554 secondary schools. A subset of the sampled schools—a total of 324 public schools representing 80 school districts nationwide—required special clearance from their districts before CAL was allowed to send questionnaires. Special clearance procedures ranged from a short request for approval from the superintendent to a very detailed research proposal that had to be approved by a committee that met every 2 months. Once permission was granted, CAL followed the same data collection procedures as for the other schools. Permission to send the survey was granted by 85% of those schools requiring special clearance.

On October 6, 2007, CAL mailed advance letters to the superintendents of the school districts of the sampled public schools, explaining the nature of the survey, listing the schools in their district that would be involved, and asking for their support. Three days later, CAL sent survey packets to the principals of all the schools, which included a short letter, the questionnaire with instructions for completing and submitting it by mail or online, and a postage-paid return envelope. The principal or foreign language teacher (at elementary schools) and foreign language chairperson or teacher (at secondary schools) were asked to complete the questionnaire within 3 weeks. A reminder packet was mailed on November 17, 2007, to schools from which a questionnaire had not yet been received. As of January 7, 2008, only 16% of sampled schools had completed a survey (Table 3). This is in contrast to the 1997 survey, when 54% of all sampled schools had responded at a similar point in time after the second mailing.

From January through June 2008, CAL staff contacted over 3,200 nonresponding schools to urge them to complete the questionnaire or to provide the survey information over the telephone. Using a detailed telephone protocol, CAL staff asked respondents whether their school taught foreign languages. If the answer was no, the respondent was asked to answer only three more questions. If the answer was yes, CAL staff either went through the questionnaire over the telephone with the school's principal, foreign language chairperson, or foreign language teacher and recorded their answers on a copy of the questionnaire, or they

Table 3. School Response Rates During Data Collection Phases

	Sample[a]	Response after first mailing	Response after second mailing	Response after final follow-up
Elementary				
Public	2,192	251	419	1,835
Private	1,190	150	166	833
Total (%)	3,382 (100)	401 (12)	585 (17)	2,668 (79)
Secondary				
Public	761	115	144	519
Private	693	49	66	483
Total (%)	1,454 (100)	164 (11)	210 (14)	1,002 (69)
Total (%)	4,836 (100)	565 (12)	795 (16)	3,670 (76)

Note. First return as of November 8, 2007; second return as of January 7, 2008.

[a]Sample number excludes out-of-scope schools.

asked the respondent to complete and submit the survey online or to complete it on paper and return it by fax or mail. In this way, a final response rate of 76% was obtained. More than half of all questionnaires (54%) were completed by telephone, 30% were submitted by mail, 15% by Web, and 1% by fax (Table 4). It was an unexpected result that the print survey was chosen by twice as many respondents as the online survey.

At the end of the data collection period, 3,670 valid questionnaires (72% of original sampled schools) had been completed and returned to CAL by principals, foreign language chairpersons, and language teachers from 2,668 elementary schools and 1,002 secondary schools. An additional 279 questionnaires (5%) were excluded from analysis for a variety of reasons (out of scope schools), including closure of school, change of school level (e.g., from elementary to secondary school), or no students in Grade 1 or above. There were 37 schools (1%) that refused to complete a survey (final refusal schools) and 1,129 schools (22%) that did not respond (no response schools). (See Table 5.)

Table 4. Modes of Questionnaire Completion and Submission

	Number of surveys	Percentage
Telephone	1,968	54%
Mail	1,087	30%
Web	557	15%
Fax	58	1%
Total surveys completed	3,670	101%[a]

[a]Total is more than 100% due to rounding.

Table 5. Final Survey Status

	Number	Percentage
Schools included in analysis	3,670	72%
Out of scope schools	279	5%
Final refusal schools	37	1%
No response schools	1,129	22%
All surveys	5,115	100%

Data Analysis Procedures

CAL and Westat conducted the data processing and analysis for the study. CAL staff reviewed each returned survey for consistency and missing information and contacted approximately 350 schools to ask for missing information or clarification. Data entry and processing were automatic for questionnaires submitted online; Westat conducted the data entry and processing for print questionnaires and produced tabulations and standard errors for all data using SAS, a computer statistical program.

Table 6. Elementary School Grade Level Combinations

	1987 (%)	1997 (%)	2008 (%)
K/1–3	5	13	3
K/1–5	18	30	34
K/1–6	29	26	19
K/1–8	20	27	20
K/1–12			9
4–6		2	1
Other[a]	29	1	15

Note. Based on weighted data; totals may not equal 100% because of rounding. Empty cells indicate no responses for those categories.

[a] In 2008, other grade levels included different combinations of grades (e.g., Grades 2–5, 1–4). Other grade levels for 1987 included any responses greater than K/1–8, combined schools, and other combinations not included above (such as preschool through Grade 3, Grades 1–4). For 1997, the responses greater than K/1–8 and combined schools were included in the K/1–8 category.

Table 7. Secondary School Grade Level Combinations

	1987 (%)	1997 (%)	2008 (%)
5–7		1	
5–8		24	3
6–8			23
7–8	10	8	
7–9[a]	6	3	9
7–12	13	12	1
9–12[b]	41	42	33
10–12	6	4	
K–12[c]		6	15
Other[d]	23	1	17

Note. Based on weighted data; totals may not equal 100% because of rounding.

[a]In 2008, included Grade 7, 7–8, 8–9.

[b]In 2008, included Grades 10–12.

[c]In 2008, included Grades 1–12, 2–12, 3–12, 4–12.

[d]Other grade levels for 1987 included Grades 5–7, 5–8, 8–9, and other combined schools, including K–12; note that in 1997 Grades 5–7, 5–8, and K–12 were assigned to separate categories.

In addition to examining overall results for 2008 survey items and comparing subgroups (e.g., by school size, region), we analyzed data from the 1997 and 2008 surveys for significant increases or decreases over time for comparable items. Westat conducted all tests for statistical significance[8] (i.e., t-tests for means and/or proportions) using weighted data and a significance level of 0.05. The SAS programs used for tabulations for the 2008 data produced standard errors that accounted for complex sampling procedures. The formula for estimating standard errors for the 1997 data also took into account the design effect (or DEFT).

Demographic Profile of Sample

Elementary Schools

As in the 1987 and 1997 surveys, elementary schools responding to the 2008 survey included schools with a wide range of grade combinations from preschool through Grade 8 (Table 6). For this survey, elementary school was defined as a school with students in Grade 4 or lower and no grade higher than Grade 8. (Note that for K–12 schools and other combined schools, respondents were asked to complete the elementary survey with reference to their school's elementary grades only.) As in the past, schools with prekindergarten were included with those that start with kindergarten. These were the most frequent grade combinations:

- Kindergarten or Grade 1 to Grade 5 (34%)
- Kindergarten or Grade 1 to Grade 8 (20%)
- Kindergarten or Grade 1 to Grade 6 (19%)

The average elementary school enrollment in 2008 was 378, compared with 394 in 1987 and 406 in 1997. However, the method for asking for enrollment differed across the three surveys. The 2008 survey asked for the exact number of students enrolled, whereas the 1987 and 1997 surveys listed categories with enrollment ranges for respondents to check; for those surveys, mean numbers were computed based on the midpoint of each category.

[8] When the terms *significance, significant,* or *statistically significant* are used in this report, it means that the differences obtained are unlikely to have occurred by chance. The significance level used for this data is 0.05 (sometimes noted as $p<.05$), which means that there is less than a 5% probability (p) that the difference between two numbers presented as statistically significant is actually not statistically significant, but happened only by chance. Note that a statistically significant difference simply means that there is statistical evidence that there is a difference; it does not mean that the difference is necessarily important, large, or significant in the traditional meaning of the word.

Table 8. Demographic Profile of Responding Elementary Schools

	1987	1997	2008
Metro status			
Rural	617 (44%)	810 (53%)	797 (30%)
Suburban	373 (26%)	309 (20%)	1,020 (38%)
Urban	359 (25%)	399 (26%)	851 (32%)
Missing data	67 (5%)	16 (1%)	0
School type			
Public	940 (66%)	1,188 (77%)	1,835 (69%)
Private	470 (33%)	342 (22%)	833 (31%)
Missing data	6 (0.4%)	4 (0.3%)	0
Public school			
Rural	473 (50%)	692 (58%)	630 (34%)
Suburban	241 (26%)	227 (19%)	679 (37%)
Urban	192 (20%)	257 (22%)	526 (29%)
Missing data	34 (4%)	12 (1%)	0
Private school			
Rural	144 (31%)	115 (34%)	167 (20%)
Suburban	132 (28%)	82 (24%)	341 (41%)
Urban	167 (36%)	141 (41%)	325 (39%)
Missing data	27 (6%)	4 (1%)	0
Total	1,416	1,534	2,668

Note. Table includes unweighted numbers. Some percentages do not equal 100% due to rounding.

Table 9. Demographic Profile of Responding Secondary Schools

	1987	1997	2008
Metro status			
Rural	647 (48%)	965 (58%)	311 (31%)
Suburban	342 (25%)	347 (21%)	364 (36%)
Urban	291 (22%)	323 (20%)	327 (33%)
Missing data	69 (5%)	15 (0.9%)	0
School type			
Public	1,033 (77%)	1,430 (87%)	519 (52%)
Private	306 (23%)	215 (13%)	483 (48%)
Missing data	10 (0.7%)	5 (0.3%)	0
Public school			
Rural	549 (53%)	873 (61%)	206 (40%)
Suburban	267 (26%)	298 (21%)	182 (35%)
Urban	180 (17%)	246 (17%)	131 (25%)
Missing data	37 (4%)	13 (0.9%)	0
Private school			
Rural	98 (32%)	89 (41%)	105 (21%)
Suburban	75 (25%)	48 (22%)	182 (38%)
Urban	111 (36%)	76 (35%)	196 (41%)
Missing data	22 (7%)	2 (0.9%)	0
Total	1,349	1,650	1,002

Note. Table includes unweighted numbers. Some percentages do not equal 100% due to rounding.

Secondary Schools[9]

At the secondary level, the most frequent grade combination was Grade 9 or 10 to Grade 12, which included 33% of all secondary schools, followed by Grade 6 to Grade 8, which included 23% of secondary schools. (See Table 7 for other grade combinations.) For this survey, middle school was defined as a school sampled as a secondary school and that included no grade higher than Grade 9. High schools were schools that included grades above Grade 9.

[9] Unless otherwise noted, the category middle school used in this report includes combination schools (schools with both elementary and secondary grades) that were sampled as secondary schools and did not include grades above Grade 9. The category high school includes combination schools with Grades 10 or higher (unless otherwise noted). It should be noted that K–8 schools were sampled as elementary schools.

In 2008, the average enrollment in secondary schools was 643, which is lower than the average estimated enrollment in 1987 (671) or 1997 (716). Some of the difference may reflect the different methodology for estimating enrollment in the two earlier surveys.

Additional Demographic Characteristics

Tables 8 and 9 provide additional demographic information from the responding samples of each of the surveys, including the number of public and private schools and the number of rural, suburban, and urban schools in total and by school type (public vs. private).

PART 3
Results

CHAPTER 3: AMOUNT OF LANGUAGE INSTRUCTION

This chapter provides results on the percentage of schools teaching foreign languages, the percentage of schools not teaching languages that were planning to offer them in the future, and nationwide enrollment in foreign language classes. These results provide key information about the prevalence of language teaching in U.S. schools. Results for each section are presented first for elementary schools and then for secondary schools. The 2008 survey results are presented along with 1987 and 1997 survey results to show trends in language education over three points in time.

Schools Offering Foreign Language Instruction

Elementary Schools

Over the past decade, the percentage of elementary schools nationwide offering foreign language instruction has decreased by 6 percentage points (Figure 1). In 1997, 31% of elementary schools offered foreign languages. By 2008, the number had fallen to 25%, a statistically significant decrease. This contrasts with an increase of 9 percentage points from 1987 to 1997, when the percentage of elementary schools offering foreign language instruction rose from 22% to 31%.

The overall decline in elementary school language instruction as of 2008 was almost entirely the result of a decrease in the percentage of public elementary schools offering foreign languages. From 1987 to 1997, the percentage of public elementary schools teaching languages increased from 17% to 24%; this upward trend was reversed from 1997 to 2008. In 2008, only 15% of public elementary schools offered foreign language instruction, a statistically significant decrease from 1997. In contrast, the percentage of private elementary schools offering language instruction remained fairly stable between 1997 and 2008, following a sizeable increase from 1987 to 1997. Thus, while only 15% of public elementary schools reported offering foreign languages in 2008, 51% of private elementary schools reported doing so.

In 2008, as in 1997, more foreign language instruction took place in suburban and urban elementary schools than in rural schools, both public and private (Table 10). Overall, 32% of suburban elementary schools and 29% of urban elementary schools offered foreign languages compared to 16% of rural elementary schools, a statistically significant difference for both suburban-rural and urban-rural comparisons. Although language instruction in all locations decreased over the past decade, the decline was steepest in rural schools: from 25% in 1997 to 16% in 2008.

Table 10. Elementary Schools Teaching Foreign Languages (by Metro Status) (2008)

	Public (%)	Private (%)	Total (%)[a]
Urban[b]	15	57	29
Suburban[b]	18	63	32
Rural[b]	11	29	16

[a] Differences were statistically significant in the Total column between urban and rural schools and between suburban and rural schools.

[b] Differences between public and private elementary schools were statistically significant for each metro status (urban, suburban, rural).

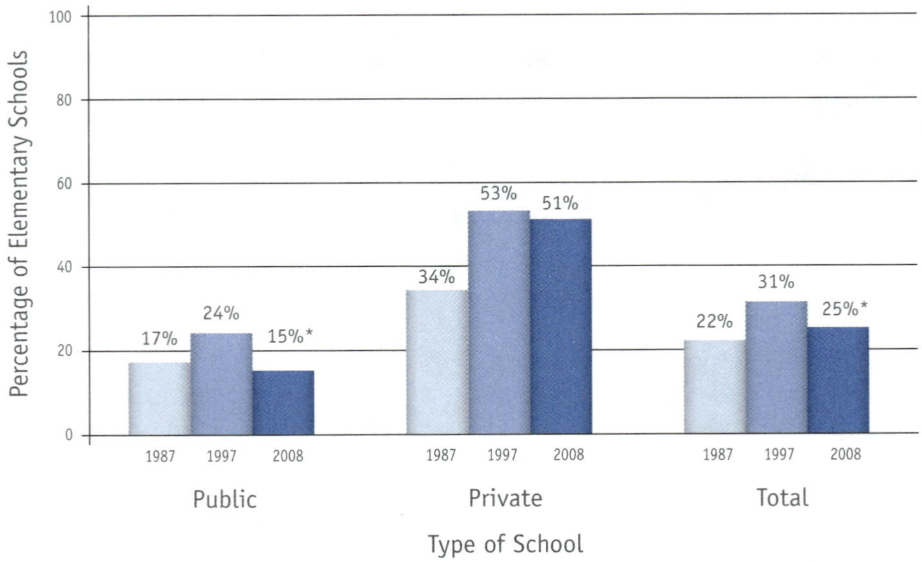

Figure 1. Elementary Schools Teaching Foreign Languages (by School Type) (1987, 1997, 2008).

*A statistically significant decrease from 1997 to 2008.

Table 11. Elementary Schools Teaching Foreign Languages (by Region) (1997, 2008)

	1997 (%)	2008 (%)
NEC (Northeast)	39	33[a]
SCOLT (South)	39	31[a]
PNCFL (Pacific Northwest)	24	25
SWCOLT (Southwest)	37	22[a,b]
CSC (Central)	25	20[a]

Note. NEC = Northeast Conference on the Teaching of Foreign Languages; SCOLT = Southern Conference on Language Teaching; PNCFL = Pacific Northwest Council for Languages; SWCOLT = Southwest Conference on Language Teaching; CSC = Central States Conference on the Teaching of Foreign Languages.

[a] Differences were statistically significant between NEC and SWCOLT, between NEC and CSC, between SCOLT and SWCOLT, and between SCOLT and CSC.

[b] Decrease in SWCOLT from 1997 to 2008 was statistically significant.

Table 12. Public Elementary Schools Teaching Foreign Languages (by Socioeconomic Status) (2008)

	Public elementary schools (%)
High SES	22[a]
Medium SES	11
Low SES	12
Very low SES	14

Note. High SES school = <20% eligible for free or reduced-price lunch; medium SES school = 20%–39% eligible; low SES school = 40%–69% eligible; very low SES school = ≥70% eligible.

[a] Differences were statistically significant between high SES schools and all other schools.

Foreign language instruction also varied across geographical regions. Regional results were compiled according to the five foreign language conference regions in order to assist the profession in regional initiatives. Elementary schools in the Northeast Conference and Southern Conference regions were significantly more likely to offer foreign languages than those in the Southwest and Central regions; the Pacific Northwest fell in the middle (Table 11). The decrease in the percentage of elementary schools offering foreign language instruction in the Southwest Conference region (from 37% to 22%) was statistically significant.

There was a direct correlation between the socioeconomic status (SES) of students at public elementary schools and the availability of foreign language instruction. High SES schools were more likely to teach foreign languages than schools in each of the other SES categories; the differences were statistically significant (Table 12).

Secondary Schools

The percentage of secondary schools teaching foreign languages also fell to a statistically significant degree from 1997 to 2008, from 86% to 79% (Figure 2). However, this drop was accounted for primarily by a decrease in foreign language instruction at the middle school level. The percentage of middle schools offering foreign language instruction decreased from 75% in 1997 to 58% in 2008, a statistically significant decrease. In contrast, high schools maintained a relatively stable level of foreign language instruction over the same period. There were no statistically significant differences from 1997 to 2008 at either public or private high schools.

As with elementary schools, the percentage of secondary schools offering foreign language instruction varied according to metro status (Table 13). For middle schools, more instruction was taking place in urban and suburban schools than in rural schools. The difference between urban and rural middle schools and the difference between suburban and rural middle schools were both statistically significant. By comparison, suburban high schools were more likely to offer foreign languages than either urban or rural high schools to a statistically significant degree.

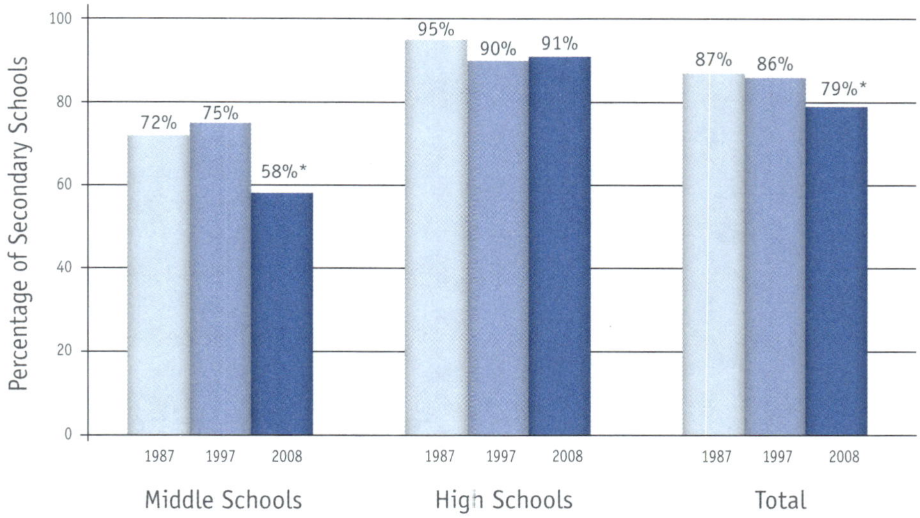

Figure 2. Secondary Schools Teaching Foreign Languages (by School Level) (1987, 1997, 2008).

Note. The majority of middle schools in the sample were public schools.

*A statistically significant decrease from 1997 to 2008.

Table 13. Secondary Schools Teaching Foreign Languages (by Metro Status and School Type) (2008)

	Public and private			Public[a]	
	All secondary schools[b] (%)	Middle schools (%)	High schools (%)	Middle schools (%)	High schools (%)
Urban	82	72	88	71	84
Suburban	84	68	96[d]	68	100
Rural	74	44[c]	90	43	91

[a]Statistical tests not conducted for metro status of public schools.

[b]Includes middle schools, high schools, and combination schools.

[c]Statistically significant difference compared to urban and suburban schools.

[d]Statistically significant difference compared to urban and rural schools.

Table 14. Secondary Schools Teaching Foreign Languages (by School Size) (2008)

	Middle school (%)[a]	High school (%)[b]
Small	29	83
Medium	68	98
Large	87	100
Very large	67	100

Note. Small school = <400 students; medium school = 400–999 students; large school = 1,000–1,399 students; very large schools = ≥1,400 students.

[a]Differences were statistically significant between small middle schools and all other size middle schools and between medium and large middle schools.

[b]Differences were statistically significant between small high schools and all other size high schools.

Table 15. Secondary Schools Teaching Foreign Languages (by Region) (1997, 2008)

	1997 (%)	2008 (%)[a]
NEC (Northeast)	94	91
SCOLT (South)	88	82
CSC (Central)	86	77
SWCOLT (Southwest)	87	76[b]
PNCFL (Pacific Northwest)	72	61

[a]Statistically significant differences between NEC and SWCOLT, NEC and CSC, NEC and PNCFL, SCOLT and PNCFL.

[b]Decrease in SWCOLT from 1997 to 2008 is statistically significant.

As in the 1997 survey, there was a direct correlation between school size and foreign language instruction (Table 14). Small middle schools and small high schools were significantly less likely to offer foreign languages than medium, large, or very large schools. At the middle school level, there was also a statistically significant difference between medium and large schools.

There was also variation in the availability of foreign language instruction across geographical regions. As in 1997, secondary schools in the Northeast Conference region were more likely to offer foreign languages than schools in any of the other regions (Table 15). The percentage of secondary schools offering foreign language instruction decreased in all conference regions over the past decade.

As in public elementary schools, there was a direct correlation between the socioeconomic status of students in public middle schools and the offering of foreign language instruction in those schools (Table 16). Middle schools with a high SES were more likely to offer foreign language instruction than middle schools with a lower SES. At the high school level, there were no statistically significant differences in the availability of foreign language instruction based on socioeconomic status.

Table 16. Secondary Schools Teaching Foreign Languages (by Socioeconomic Status) (2008)

	Middle school (%)[a]	High school (%)	All schools (%)[b]
High SES	74	94	87
Medium SES	64	100	82
Low SES	47	92	69
Very low SES	45	75	60

Note. High SES school = <20% eligible for free or reduced-price lunch; medium SES school = 20%–39% eligible; low SES school = 40%–69% eligible; very low SES school = ≥70% eligible.

[a]Differences were statistically significant between high SES middle schools and low and very low SES middle schools and between medium SES middle schools and low SES middle schools.

[b]For all secondary schools, differences were statistically significant between high SES schools and low and very low SES schools and between medium SES schools and low and very low SES schools.

Schools Planning to Offer Foreign Language Instruction

Elementary Schools

Of those elementary schools surveyed that did not teach foreign languages during the school day, only 8% reported that they were planning to offer foreign languages in the next 2 years. There was more interest among private elementary schools than public (Figure 3).[10]

[10] Because of a change in wording in an attempt to obtain more useful data, the data for this question are not comparable to the data for a related question in earlier surveys. (The 2008 question was "Is your school planning to offer foreign language instruction in the next two years?" while the earlier question was, "Would you like to start foreign language instruction at your school?") It is interesting to note, however, the strong interest in the past in starting new programs. In 1997, 54% of elementary schools that did not teach foreign language reported that they would be interested in starting language instruction at their school.

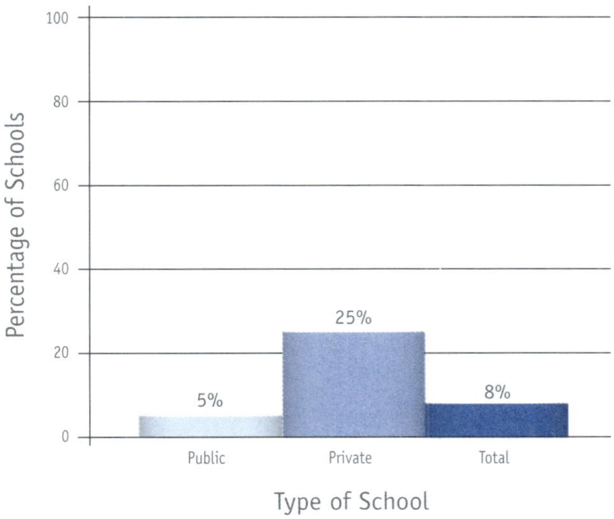

Figure 3. Elementary Schools Not Currently Teaching Foreign Languages but Planning to Offer Them (by School Type) (2008).

Many respondents (205) from schools that did not offer foreign languages offered comments about their response to this question.[11] Of those who provided comments, 14% were from schools that reported planning to teach a foreign language in the next 2 years, and 86% were from schools that were not planning to teach a foreign language in the next 2 years.

Of the 14% of respondents who stated they had plans to teach a foreign language, the answers ran from the definite—"We are adding Spanish next year" (California)—to the possible—"We are trying to offer Japanese" (Hawaii). This is to say that the yes responses were not all definite. Likewise, the schools' plans for future programs differed:

> "We are looking at offering other methods of instruction (e.g., Rosetta Stone). We're looking at Chinese, Spanish, Gaelic conversation." (California)

> "Pilot program for K-1 starting this semester." (Ohio)

> "Each year it depends. Foreign language is offered as an elective." (Texas)

> "We will teach Spanish next year – we will start a dual language program in kindergarten." (Idaho)

Among the 86% of respondents who answered that they were not planning to offer languages in the next 2 years, there were some definite *nos*, for example, "Never!" (California) and "Not to students, no" (California). Many of the comments cited similar reasons for not planning to offer languages:

- Funding issues
- District-level decision making that prevents the school from deciding whether to offer foreign languages
- Languages not seen as a core component of an elementary school curriculum
- Previously existing program no longer feasible
- Shortage of foreign language teachers
- Extracurricular foreign language instruction available
- Other (e.g., uncertainty, particular circumstances of the school or state)

Some of the specific comments received in each category from schools not planning to offer languages are provided below.

Funding

Budget constraints were mentioned as a reason for not being able to offer foreign language instruction by 12% of the schools that provided comments:

> "We do not have the financial resources." (Wisconsin)

> "Spanish teaching stopped two years ago due to budget cuts (in the millions). Over 300-400

[11] It is interesting to note that although respondents were not asked to provide comments to this question (and there was no place to do so), many felt compelled to provide more of a response. Those completing paper copies of the survey scribbled their comments on the margins while those responding to the survey by telephone volunteered comments. Respondents who submitted their surveys online, however, did not have the opportunity to provide comments to this question.

teachers in the district might not have jobs next year due to the deficit." (California)

"It is possible, we have in the past. It depends on funding." (Kansas)

"We hope to, but no funding." (Louisiana)

Decisions Made at the District Level
Thirteen percent of the respondents commented that they had little say in whether languages could be offered because the decision was made at the district level:

"Would love to have it, but no one is available. The decision is made by the central office." (Tennessee)

"No, because we are with the [ ] County Public Schools and their curriculum doesn't include foreign language." (Maryland)

"It's a bush school (teachers fly in). You need to call the district office to find out." (Alaska)

Languages Not Seen as Core Component of Curriculum
Four percent of comment providers explained that foreign languages were not viewed as a core component of an elementary school curriculum:

"It is not customary to teach foreign language at the elementary level, I don't think." (Washington)

"I don't think so, it's an elementary school." (Hawaii)

"Not in grammar school." (North Carolina)

"Usually they wait until middle school for that." (Wisconsin)

"We don't teach languages in our school or in our community at the elementary level." (Arizona)

"We don't teach foreign language, we're an elementary school." (California)

Previously Existing Language Program No Longer Feasible
Seven percent of comment providers mentioned that their schools had previously taught foreign language but that they did not plan to do so again in the near future.

"Last year we had French, but the teacher moved." (Wisconsin)

"We have taught foreign language in the past but it didn't work out this year." (Pennsylvania)

"We used to teach foreign language, but we don't anymore." (Georgia)

"We offered foreign language in the past, but the teacher was a volunteer and she left, so now there is no time or money." (Wisconsin)

Shortage of Foreign Language Teachers
Lack of available foreign language teachers resonated as an explicit concern for 6% of those who provided comments:

"It would depend on finding a Zuni teacher. Three or four years ago we had one." (New Mexico)

"We taught Spanish for two years, lost the teacher, and will teach it again if a new teacher is found." (Illinois)

"No, because we don't have a teacher." (Arizona)

Extracurricular Foreign Language Instruction Available
All respondents who provided comments here had answered *no* to the survey question "Does your school currently teach foreign language(s)?" By definition, this meant that they did not offer language classes as part of the curriculum during the school day. However, 28% of the respondents providing comments

said that they currently offered some type of foreign language instruction—but presumably not during the regular school day or not taught throughout the school year. The type of program described in most of these schools was a before- or afterschool program:

> "After school Spanish voluntary program, 'Culture Kids.'" (Pennsylvania)

> "After school there's someone who comes and teaches Spanish for students who pay for it." (New York)

> "We have an active PTO that runs classes after school, and a private cultural society runs classes in Mandarin after school. There are fees involved, but scholarships are available." (Washington)

Other

Of those who provided comments, 29% expressed uncertainty about implementing a language program and described particular circumstances in their school or state:

> "Don't think we will. We're not staffed anymore. Eight to ten years ago we had a foreign language program." (California)

> "Unsure. We had foreign language in the past but it was discontinued." (Georgia)

> "Unsure. It is a topic of discussion." (Washington)

> "We're talking about teaching Dakota. We're planning to get the process going." (North Dakota)

Secondary Schools

As shown in Figure 4, 17% of the secondary schools not currently teaching foreign languages said they were planning to offer languages in the next 2 years. As with the elementary schools, there was more interest among private than public secondary schools. There was little difference between school levels: 17% of middle schools and 18% of high schools said they were planning to offer languages in the next 2 years. Because of the change in question wording described earlier, 2008 data could not be compared to data from the previous surveys. It is interesting to note, however, the strong interest reported in 1997 in starting new programs: 68% of secondary schools that did not teach foreign languages at the time reported that they would be interested in starting language instruction at their school.

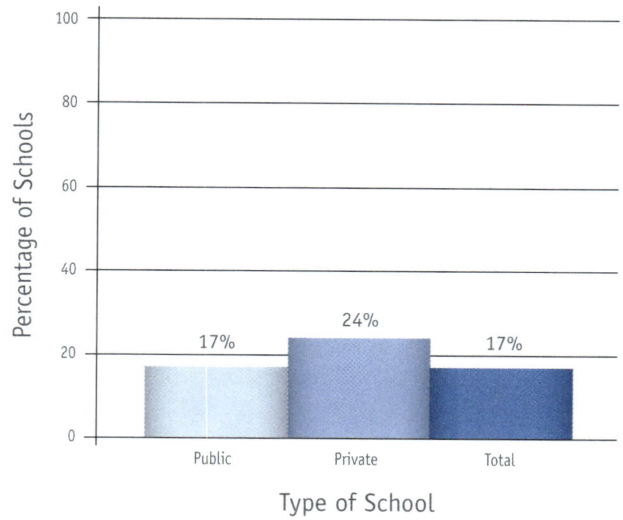

Figure 4. Secondary Schools Not Currently Teaching Foreign Languages but Planning to Offer Them (by School Type) (2008).

Students Enrolled in Foreign Language Classes

Elementary Schools

In 2008, an estimated 4.2 million elementary school students in the United States, out of 27.5 million (15%), were enrolled in foreign language classes at school.[12] Between 1997 and 2008, the number of public elementary school students enrolled in foreign language classes declined from 2.5 to 2.2 million, while the number of private elementary school students enrolled in foreign language classes increased from 1.5 million to almost 2 million. Within the public elementary schools that offered foreign languages in 2008, 67% of students were enrolled in foreign language classes, up from 50% in 1997.[13] Within the private elementary schools that offered foreign languages in 2008, 78% of students were enrolled in foreign language classes, which is similar to the percentage reported in 1997.

Secondary Schools

At the secondary school level, an estimated 10.5 million U.S. students out of 25.7 million (41%) were enrolled in foreign language classes at school in 2008, a decline from the nearly 12 million (52%) enrolled in 1997. Of the students enrolled in foreign languages in 2008, about 2.3 million were in middle schools or junior high schools, 6.7 million were in high schools, and 1.5 million were in combined junior/senior high schools. Approximately 84% of secondary students enrolled in foreign languages were in public schools. Within public middle schools that offered foreign languages, 36% of all students were enrolled in foreign language classes; there were too few private middle schools for reliable estimates.[14] Within high schools that offered foreign language classes, 48% of public school students and 73% of private school students were enrolled in them.

Discussion

Survey results show that, whereas high schools maintained a stable level of foreign language instruction over the past decade, the percentage of elementary and middle schools offering foreign language instruction decreased significantly from 1997 to 2008. The number of students enrolled in foreign language classes also decreased.[15] Indeed, with only 25% of elementary schools and 58% of middle schools offering foreign languages, the majority of students in the United States are not even given the opportunity to study a foreign language before middle school and many not until they reach high school. This situation does not seem likely to improve anytime soon: Only 8% of elementary schools that did not teach foreign languages in 2008 reported plans to offer language instruction in the next 2 years. This is in stark contrast with the surge of new language programs implemented in elementary schools in the 1980s and 1990s (Heining-Boynton, 1990; Taboada, 2004; Viadero, 1991).

Major issues, such as limited funding and a shortage of qualified teachers, were reported as factors in deciding whether to offer foreign language instruction in elementary schools. Another often mentioned factor was that languages are not considered part of the core curriculum for elementary school students. Interest in starting language instruction among secondary schools not currently teaching languages was also low, but perhaps for different reasons. For example, a recent study, conducted by the Language Learning Center of the University of Washington (2008), which looked at high schools in Washington that did not offer languages, found that most students were able to take

[12] Because a sizeable minority of schools did not provide data on the number of students enrolled in foreign languages, the total foreign language enrollment was estimated as follows: The mean enrollment was calculated for those schools that provided enrollment data, then the mean was multiplied by the number of schools offering foreign languages. This implicit imputation assumes that the mean foreign language enrollment among schools not providing data is similar to the mean foreign language enrollment among those that did. This is just one of many alternative ways that the missing values could be imputed. Other methods may lead to different estimates. Given the extent of missing enrollment data (22% of elementary schools and 34% of secondary schools), estimates using the imputed values are subject to biases of unknown magnitude. In addition, the method of calculating enrollment (both total enrollment and enrollment in foreign languages) varied between the 1997 and 2008 surveys. In 2008, we asked respondents to provide total enrollment figures, whereas in 1997, we provided enrollment ranges and asked respondents to indicate the range in which their school's enrollment fell; total enrollment was then calculated by multiplying the number of schools teaching foreign languages by the midpoint of the category. Although this is a reasonable way of estimating enrollment, it assumes that the average is the midpoint of the category, which it may not be. So some of the differences in estimates may be attributable to the different means of calculation, as well as to the amount of missing data.

[13] Based on schools that provided both total enrollment and enrollment in foreign languages.

[14] Private middle schools are extremely rare. There were only 10 in the sample, of which 7 offered foreign languages.

[15] While the data collected make it possible to estimate student enrollment in foreign language classes nationwide, it has to be cautioned that both the enrollment numbers and the observed trends are subject to limitations because of different computation methods used for the 1997 and 2008 enrollment estimates and the impact of missing data on overall estimates. This points to the need for more complete and accurate enrollment data collection at the local, state, and national levels.

language classes elsewhere. Their options included taking classes at other high schools in the area, at local community colleges, through online programs, or through a combination of these options. This shows that the absence of foreign language instruction at a particular high school does not necessarily mean that students are not studying languages at all.

The results of CAL's survey also point to an issue of unequal access to foreign language instruction. Schools with higher SES students and those located in urban and suburban areas were more likely to offer languages. In addition, the percentage of private elementary schools that offered foreign language instruction was three times the percentage of public elementary schools that did.

School size also affected the offering of languages. At the secondary level, smaller schools were significantly less likely than larger schools to offer foreign languages. Larger schools are typically able to offer a wider range of courses, including languages, because of the larger number of students and teachers.

After analyzing the data from the 1997 survey, CAL researchers predicted that "the number of elementary and secondary language programs will increase... [to] allow students to attain the proficiency needed to communicate and participate in our increasingly interconnected world" (Rhodes & Branaman, 1999, p. 65). Unfortunately, this anticipated increase has not taken place. On the contrary, the number of language programs in U.S. schools decreased at the same time that much of the rest of the world was moving in the other direction—providing quality language instruction to students throughout their schooling (Education, Audiovisual & Culture Executive Agency, 2008; Pufahl, Rhodes, & Christian, 2000).

Unless foreign language teaching is recognized as an important priority for the nation, the decline in the number of U.S. public schools offering languages is likely to continue. Furthermore, access to foreign language instruction could eventually be limited primarily to students in high SES schools in urban and suburban districts. Given that most selective colleges and universities expect incoming students to have studied a foreign language, our K–12 education system appears to be increasing the gap between the privileged and the underprivileged.

CHAPTER 4: LANGUAGES, PROGRAM TYPES, AND SCHEDULING

This chapter presents survey results on the specific languages taught in schools, the types of programs or classes offered, the grade and course levels at which foreign language instruction is offered, the number of hours or minutes of instruction provided per week, and the number of weeks of instruction offered each year. These results show important trends in the languages offered to students and in the type and amount of instruction provided. Results for each section are presented first for elementary schools, then for secondary schools. The discussion section provides an analysis of the data in the context of current trends in foreign language education.

Languages Offered

Elementary Schools

Spanish continued to be the most commonly taught language in elementary schools and increased in popularity over the last 20 years (Table 17 and Figure 5). In 2008, Spanish was taught at 88% of elementary schools that offered language instruction, compared to 79% in 1997—a statistically significant increase. The increase from 1987 (68%) to 1997 was also statistically significant. The increase over the past decade was driven primarily by private schools: The percentage of private elementary schools offering Spanish increased from 77% to 92%, compared to an increase from 80% to 82% in public schools.

Chinese, Latin, and Arabic also rose from a decade ago, although these languages were still taught at few schools. There was a statistically significant increase in the percentage of elementary schools teaching Chinese, from 0.3% of schools with foreign language programs in 1997 to 3% in 2008. Chinese was offered at a higher percentage of private schools (4% of those offering languages) than public schools (2%). Latin instruction increased from 3% to 6% of elementary schools that offered languages, which was not a statistically significant increase. As with Chinese, Latin was offered at a higher percentage of private schools (9% of those with language programs) than public schools (1%). Arabic also showed a small upturn, although not statistically significant, from less than 0.1% to 1% of elementary schools offering languages. There was no difference in public/private school Arabic offerings.

The teaching of French and German, on the other hand, decreased significantly. Of elementary schools offering foreign language instruction, 11% taught French in 2008, down from 27% in 1997 and 41% in 1987. The decrease over both time periods was statistically significant. The decrease from 1997 to 2008 was statistically significant for both public schools (from 27% to 8%) and private schools (from 27% to 13%). Only 2% of elementary schools teaching languages offered German in 2008, down from 5% in 1997 and 10% in 1987. This decrease was statistically significant, as was the decrease for public schools alone (from 7% to 0.7%). Private schools, however, showed a slight increase, from 2% to 3%.

Spanish continued to be the most commonly taught language.

Table 17. Languages Offered by Elementary Schools With Foreign Language Programs (1987, 1997, 2008)

	1987	1997			2008		
	Total (%)	Public (%)	Private (%)	Total (%)	Public (%)	Private (%)	Total (%)
Spanish	68	80	77	79	82	92	88
French	41	27	27	27	8	13	11
Latin	12	1	6	3	1	9	6
Chinese	3	1	-	0.3	2	4	3
German	10	7	2	5	0.7	3	2
American Sign Language (ASL)	<1	3	1	2	-	3	2
Italian		1	3	2	2	1	2
Hebrew	6	-	4	2	-	2	1
Japanese		2	6	3	1	2	1
Arabic		-	0.1	<0.1	1	1	1
Native American languages[a]	1	1	-	1			0.6
Greek	1	-	1	1			0.4
Portuguese							0.3
Hawaiian		0.3	-	0.2			0.3
Korean							0.2
Russian	2	1	-	1	-	0.4	0.2
Yiddish							0.05
Afrikaans							0.2
Languages for native speakers							
Spanish	1	13	3	8	16	0.1	7
Arabic							<1
Chinese		1	-	0.3			<1
Greek							<1
Haitian Creole							<1
Native American Languages (Hupa, Navajo, Salish, Yup'ik)							<1

Note. Totals equal more than 100% because some schools offered more than one language. Blank cells indicate that no responses were given for those categories. A dash (-) indicates that the *n* was too small to calculate a percentage. Note that seven languages (Dutch, Filipino, Kutenai, Micronesian, Polish, Swedish, and Yagui) were taught at 0.1% or fewer schools with language programs in 1997 but did not appear in the 2008 survey. Also, five languages for native speakers (Cherokee, French, Korean, Russian, and Tewa) were taught at 0.2% or fewer schools in 1997 but did not appear in the 2008 survey.

[a]Native American languages listed by respondents in 1997 included Arapaho, Athabascan, Cherokee, Hidatsa, Navajo, Seminole, and an unspecified American Indian language. In 2008, languages included Hupa, Navajo, and Yup'ik.

Spanish for Spanish speakers, when viewed as a separate language offering, continued to rank third—after Spanish and French—in the percentage of schools offering languages. Taught by 7% of elementary schools with language programs in 2008, the percentage of schools offering Spanish for Spanish speakers remained essentially unchanged from 1997.

The following languages were offered at 1% to 2% of the elementary schools that offered foreign language instruction: American Sign Language, Italian, Hebrew, Japanese, and Arabic. Languages taught at fewer than 1% of schools with foreign language programs were Afrikaans, Greek, Hawaiian, Korean, Native American Languages (Hupa, Navajo, and Yup'ik), Portuguese, Russian, and Yiddish. Languages for native speakers taught at fewer than 1% of schools with language programs were Arabic, Chinese, Greek, Haitian Creole, and Native American Languages (Hupa, Navajo, Salish, and Yup'ik).[16]

[16] Results for all languages taught by schools are presented. However, it should be noted that those languages taught by 6% or fewer schools have a larger range of error because of the small *n*s so those data are not as accurate as those for the languages represented by higher percentages.

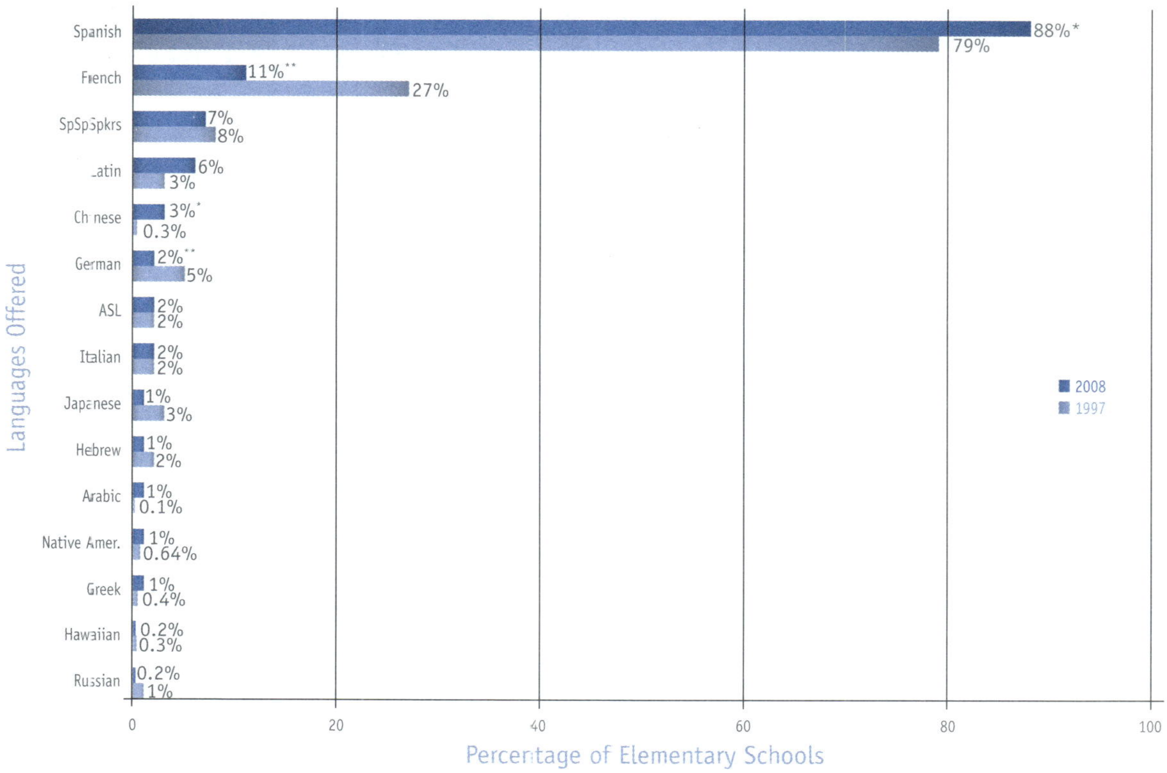

Figure 5. Languages Offered by Elementary Schools With Foreign Language Programs (1997, 2008).

Note. SpSpSpkrs = Spanish for Spanish speakers; ASL = American Sign Language. Native Amer. = Native American languages.

* Indicates a statistically significant increase from 1997 to 2008.

** Indicates a statistically significant decrease from 1997 to 2008.

To summarize, there was a statistically significant increase in the percentage of all elementary schools teaching Spanish and Chinese, as well as in the percentage of private schools teaching Spanish. There was a statistically significant decrease in the percentage of elementary schools (all schools, public schools, and private schools) teaching French, as well as in the percentage of public elementary schools teaching German.

In each of the five conference regions, Spanish was taught in 80% or more of the elementary schools offering foreign languages. The Central region reported the highest percentage of Spanish, at 93%. The Northeast had the highest percentage of French instruction, followed by the Pacific Northwest and Southern regions. Spanish for Spanish speakers was taught most frequently in the Southwestern and Pacific Northwest regions; German was taught somewhat more frequently in the Southwest than in the other regions. Latin was taught most in the South and Northeast (Table 18).

Secondary Schools

Spanish continued to be the most commonly taught language in secondary schools; it was taught at 93% of secondary schools that offered foreign language instruction. The percentage of secondary schools teaching Spanish remained steady over the last decade, after experiencing a statistically significant increase

Table 18. Top Six Languages Offered by Elementary Schools (by Region) (1997, 2008)

	NEC (Northeast)		SCOLT (South)		SWCOLT (Southwest)		CSC (Central)		PNCFL (Pacific Northwest)	
	1997 (%)	2008 (%)	1997 (%)	2008 (%)	1997 (%)	2008 (%)	1997 (%)	2008 (%)	1997 (%)	2008 (%)
Spanish	77	88	74	88	95	81	72	93	89	80
French	39	22	35	10	5	5	31	7	6	12
Spanish for Spanish Speakers	4	2	9	5	19	15	4	4	15	14
Latin	4	7	6	8	1	4	3	4	0.4	4
Chinese	—	3	—	1	—	5	—	4	—	3
German	1	2	2	2	3	3	10	2	5	1

Note. Totals for each region equal more than 100% because some schools offered more than one language. A dash (—) indicates that the *n* was too small to calculate a percentage.

the previous decade (from 86% in 1987 to 93% in 1997). The teaching of the next three most commonly taught languages—French, German, and Latin—decreased over the past decade, as did the teaching of Japanese, currently ranked ninth.

French, the second most commonly taught language in secondary schools, experienced a statistically significant decline (for all schools, public schools, and private schools). From 1987 to 1997, French registered only a slight decline (from 66% to 64%), but by 2008 only 46% of secondary schools with language programs reported teaching French. Following this downward trend, German showed a statistically significant decrease from 1997 to 2008 (from 24% to 14%) as did Latin (from 20% to 13%) and Japanese (from 7% to 3%). These decreases were statistically significant for all schools, public schools, and private schools.

Chinese, on the other hand, was the only language with a statistically significant increase. Chinese instruction rose from 1% of all secondary schools offering languages in 1997 to 4% in 2008, with a higher percentage of private schools (7%) than public schools (4%) offering Chinese. (See Table 19 and Figure 6 for relevant data.) The increase was significant in all three categories for which statistical tests were conducted: all schools, public schools, and private schools.

Other languages taught by 4% or fewer of secondary schools with language programs included American Sign Language, Italian, Japanese, Hebrew, Native American Languages (Choctaw and Navajo), Greek, and Arabic. The remaining languages, taught at fewer than 0.6% of schools that offer language instruction, were Turkish, Korean, Russian, Farsi, Hmong, Panjabi, Polish, Portuguese, Tagalog, Yiddish, Hawaiian, and Ukrainian.

Language instruction for native speakers of the language continued to be offered by some secondary schools in 2008. Spanish for native speakers was the most common, offered by 8% of secondary schools that taught languages, down slightly from 9% in 1997. Instruction for native speakers of other languages—Old Russian, O'odam, Polish, Chinese, and Hawaiian—was reported by fewer than 1% of the schools offering language instruction.

The languages offered in secondary schools varied by region (Table 20). In each of the five regions, Spanish was taught in more than 90% of the secondary schools offering language instruction, with the Southwest reporting the highest percentage (95%). As was true a decade ago, French was taught most frequently in the Northeast (70%) and least frequently in the Southwest (35%). German was still taught more frequently in the Central region than in other regions; Latin was still taught more often in the Northeastern and Southern regions; and Spanish for Spanish speakers was still taught more often in the Southwest region. Because of the overall decline in French, German, and Latin instruction, each region experienced a decline over the past decade in the percentage of schools teaching those languages.

Table 19. Languages Offered by Secondary Schools With Foreign Language Programs (1987, 1997, 2008)

	1987	1997					2008				
	Total (%)	Publ. (%)	Priv. (%)	M.S. (%)	High (%)	Total (%)	Publ. (%)	Priv. (%)	M.S. (%)	High (%)	Total (%)
Spanish	86	92	100	83	99	93	94	89	94	93	93
French	66	62	71	50	77	64	49	35	39	48	46
German	28	25	19	10	35	24	15	11	9	17	14
Latin	20	16	41	6	23	20	9	27	3	17	13
Chinese	<1	1	1	0.1	2	1	4	7	2	5	4
American Sign Language	1	2	4	0.4	3	2	4	4	-	5	4
Italian	3	3	3	2	4	3	4	3	5	4	4
Japanese	1	7	11	3	11	7	3	3	0.8	4	3
Hebrew	2	0.2	1	-	0.2	0.2	0.2	4	0.1	1	1
Native American languages[a]	<1	0.1	-	0.1	-	0.1					0.8
Greek	1	-	3	-	1	1					0.7
Arabic		-	-	-	0.1	-	-	3	0.3	0.7	0.6
Turkish											0.5
Korean											0.4
Russian	2	3	3	1	5	3	0.1	0.9	-	0.4	0.3
Farsi											0.2
Hmong											0.1
Panjabi											0.1
Polish											0.1
Portuguese	<1	0.1	0.2	-	0.2	0.1	-	0.6	-	0.2	0.1
Tagalog											0.1
Yiddish											0.1
Hawaiian	<1	0.1	0.1	-	0.1	0.1					0.05
Ukrainian											0.02
Languages for native speakers											
Spanish	<1	10	5	10	10	9	10	4	7	9	8
Old Russian											0.4
O'odam											0.4
Polish		0.2	-	-	0.4	0.2					0.1
Chinese		1	-	0.2	1	0.4					0.02
Hawaiian		-	-	-	-	0.1					0.01

Note. Totals equal more than 100% because some schools offered more than one language. Blank cells indicate that no responses were given. A dash (-) indicates that the *n* was too small to calculate a percentage. Note that four languages that were taught at 0.2% or fewer schools with language programs in 1997 did not appear in the 2008 survey: Esperanto, Finnish, Sanskrit, and Tlingit. Also, eight languages for native speakers that were taught at 0.2% or fewer schools in 1997 did not appear in the 2008 survey: French, French Creole, German, Hebrew, Japanese, Navajo, Vietnamese, and Yup'ik. High = High school; M.S. = Middle School; Priv. = Private; Publ. = Public.

[a]Native American languages listed by respondents in 1997 were Navajo, Ojibwa, Shoshone, and Ute. In 2008, the languages listed were Choctaw and Navajo.

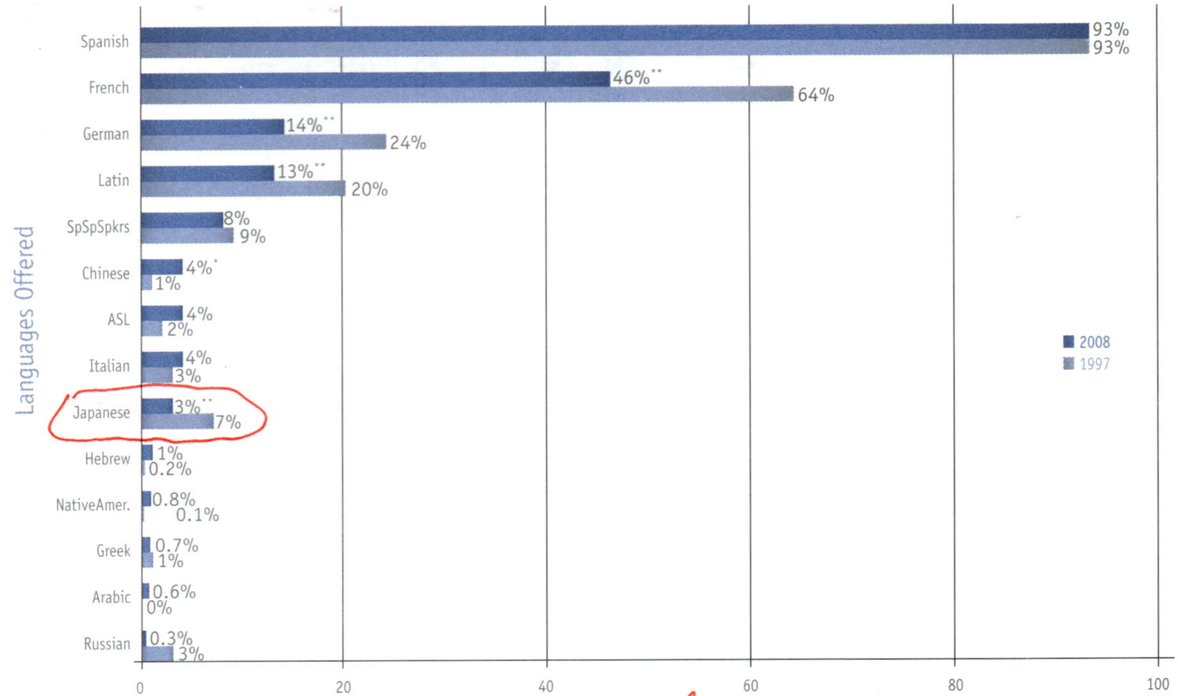

Figure 6. Languages Offered by Secondary Schools With Foreign Language Programs (1997, 2008).

Note. SpSpSpkrs = Spanish for Spanish speakers; ASL = American Sign Language; NativeAmer. = Native American languages.

* Indicates a statistically significant increase from 1997 to 2008.
** Indicates a statistically significant decrease from 1997 to 2008.

Table 20. Top Six Languages Offered by Secondary Schools (by Region) (1997, 2008)

	NEC (Northeast)		SCOLT (South)		SWCOLT (Southwest)		CSC (Central)		PNCFL (Pacific Northwest)	
	1997 (%)	2008 (%)	1997 (%)	2008 (%)	1997 (%)	1997 (%)	1997 (%)	2008 (%)	1997 (%)	2008 (%)
Spanish	100	92	89	93	94	95	91	94	95	91
French	93	70	66	40	45	35	59	43	47	36
German	27	13	14	6	29	12	30	22	15	13
Latin	36	22	24	19	12	7	14	9	12	5
Spanish for Spanish Speakers	6	7	6	8	20	18	4	3	20	3
Chinese	—	5	—	5	—	5	—	3	—	—

Note. Totals for each region equal more than 100% because many schools offer more than one language. A dash (–) indicates that the *n* was too small to calculate a percentage.

Table 21. Elementary School Foreign Language Program Types (by School Type) (2008)

	Public (%) (*N* = 230)	Private (%) (*N* = 534)	Total (%) (*N* = 764)
Exploratory	47	42	44
Language focus	39	56	50
Immersion	14	2	6

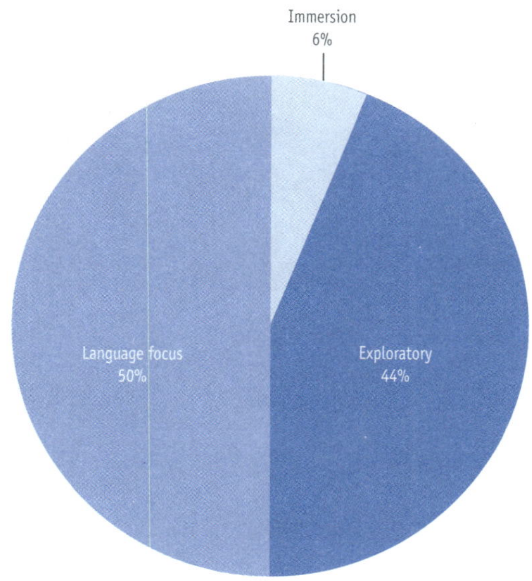

Figure 7. Elementary School Foreign Language Program Types (2008).

Program Types

Elementary Schools

To glean information about the goals and intensity of schools' language programs, the survey asked respondents to indicate, for each language offered, whether their program would best be described as exploratory, language focus, or immersion. The following definitions were provided:

> **Exploratory goals:** Gain general exposure to language and culture, learn basic words and phrases, and/or develop an interest in foreign language for future study. Portions of this program may be taught in English. (Often called *FLEX*—foreign language experience/exploratory.)

> **Language focus goals:** Acquire listening, speaking, reading, and writing skills; gain an understanding of and appreciation for other cultures. Focus of instruction can be on language and/or subject content. (Often called *FLES*—foreign language in the elementary school.)

> **Immersion goals:** Be able to communicate in the language with a high level of proficiency and acquire an understanding of and appreciation for other cultures. At least 50% of the school day is taught in the foreign language, including academic subjects. (Called *partial, total,* or *two-way immersion*, depending on the amount of foreign language used and the make-up of the student body.)

The program definitions in the 1987 and 1997 surveys were slightly different and included a fourth category, *intensive FLES,* which was subsumed under *language focus* for the 2008 survey.

In 2008, 50% of the elementary school language programs were categorized by the schools as language focus, 44% as exploratory, and 6% as immersion (Table 21, Figure 7). There were no statistically significant changes in these percentages from 1997 to 2008.

One finding was consistent over all three survey periods: More than 40% of elementary programs aimed at only introductory exposure to language in an exploratory-type program (Table 22). A contrast was noted between public and private schools in 2008: Public schools had a higher percentage of exploratory and immersion programs than private schools, whereas private schools had a higher percentage of language focus programs than public schools (Figure 8).

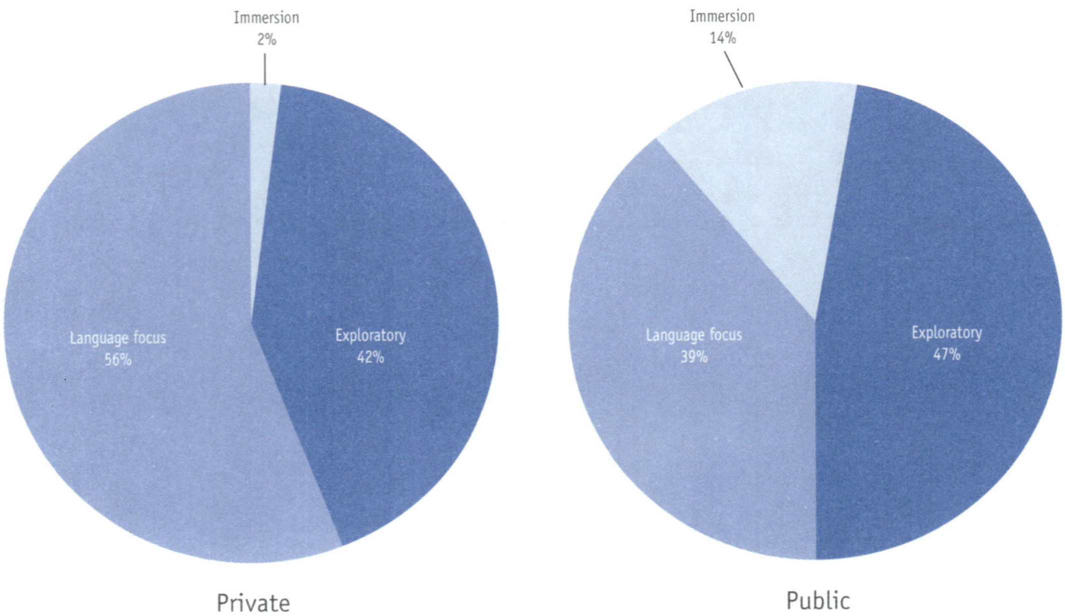

Figure 8. Elementary School Foreign Language Program Types (by School Type) (2008).

Table 22. Elementary School Foreign Language Program Types (1987, 1997, 2008)

	1987 (%) (*N* = 426)	1997 (%) (*N* = 694)	2008 (%) (*N* = 764)
Exploratory	41	45	44
Language focus[a]	57	47	50
Immersion	2	8	6

Note. N = number of programs; some schools had more than one program type. No statistical significance tests were conducted on the 1987 to 1997 data. Changes from 1997 to 2008 were not statistically significant. Only the immersion programs and an unknown percentage of language focus programs designate language proficiency as an outcome.

[a]For 1987 and 1997, the category Language focus is a combination of FLES and intensive FLES.

Secondary Schools

As in the two previous surveys, almost all secondary schools with foreign language programs in 2008 offered standard foreign language classes, which included listening, speaking, reading, writing, and culture. Other types of classes were offered at few schools. However, continuing a trend from the two previous decades, there was a statistically significant increase in the percentage of schools offering Advanced Placement (AP) classes: 21% of secondary schools with a language program offered AP language classes in 2008 compared to 16% in 1997 and 12% in 1987. Other program types that increased from 1987 to 2008 were classes for native speakers, distance learning classes, and International Baccalaureate (IB) classes (Figure 9). (The latter two categories were not listed as options in 1987 or 1997, but respondents included them under Other.) All other types of language classes remained relatively stable over the two decades, including exploratory classes, honors or accelerated classes, conversation-only classes, literature-only classes, and academic subjects taught in the foreign language.

As expected, program types varied considerably by school level. AP classes were offered almost exclusively at the high school level; 41% of all high schools with language programs reported teaching AP language classes. However, urban and suburban high schools were much more likely to offer AP classes than rural high schools (Table 23).

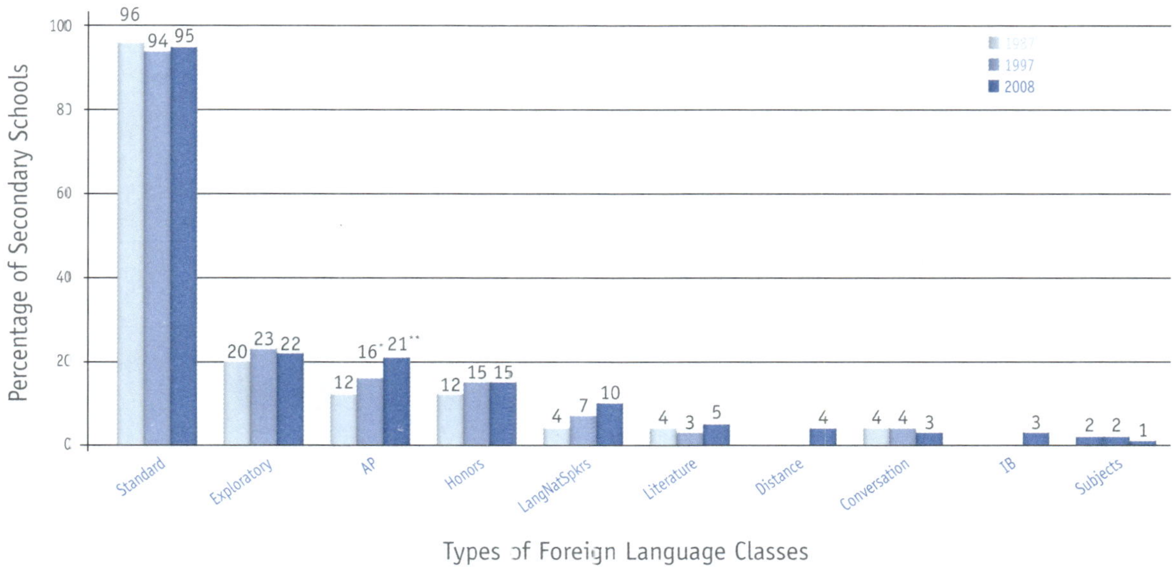

Figure 9. Secondary School Foreign Language Class Types (1987, 1997, 2008).

Note. AP = Advanced Placement; IB = International Baccalaureate; LangNatSpkrs = classes for native speakers. IB and Distance (learning) classes were not listed as options in 1987 or 1997.

* Statistically significant increase from 1987 to 1997.
** Statistically significant increase from 1997 to 2008.

Table 23. Advanced Placement Language Classes in High Schools (by Metro Status) (2008)

	Public (%)	Private (%)	All (%)
Urban	61	44	57
Suburban	54	48	54
Rural	19	22	19
Total	41	40	41

There was a correlation between each of four variables (school size, geographic region, SES, and minority enrollment) and the offering of AP language classes. The larger the school, the more likely it was to offer AP language classes. Percentages ranged from 68% of very large schools to 13% of small schools (Figure 10). High schools in the Southwest, Southern, and Northeast conference regions were more likely to offer AP classes than those in the Central and Pacific Northwest regions (Figure 11). Schools with high SES students (data available for public schools only) were more likely to offer AP classes than schools with lower SES students (Figure 12). Schools with a higher percentage of minority students were also more likely to offer AP language classes (Figure 13): 60% of the schools with very high minority enrollment offered AP language classes compared to 26% of schools with low minority enrollment. One possible explanation for this is the large number of heritage language speakers enrolled in AP language and literature classes. Heritage language speakers account for 95% of AP Chinese test takers, 60% of AP Spanish language test takers, and 80% of AP Spanish literature test takers (College Board, 2009).

Language classes for native speakers, overwhelmingly Spanish, were most likely to be offered in large public high schools, urban public high schools, low SES schools, schools in the Southwest, and schools with a high percentage of minority students. Although only 1% of the schools with language programs offered academic subjects taught in other languages,

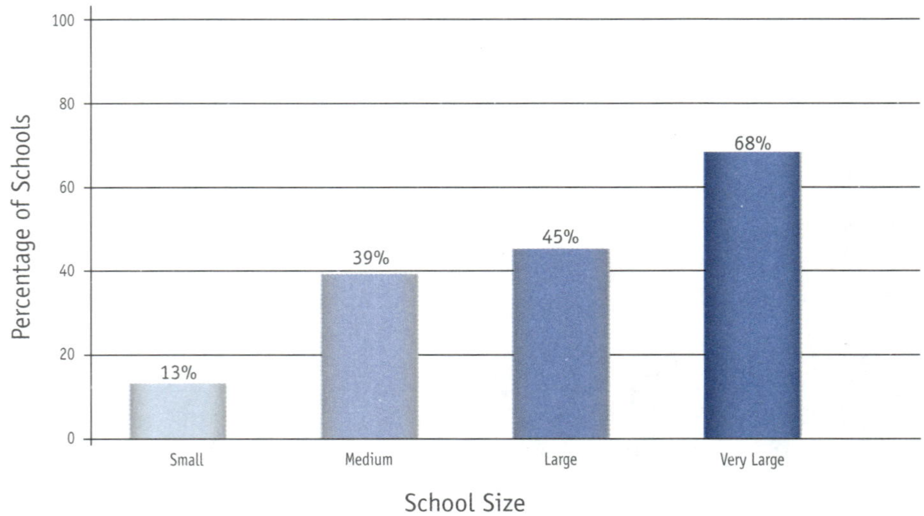

Figure 10. Advanced Placement Language Classes in High Schools (by School Size) (2008).

Note. Small school = <400 students; medium school = 400–999 students; large school = 1,000–1,399 students; very large school = ≥1,400 students.

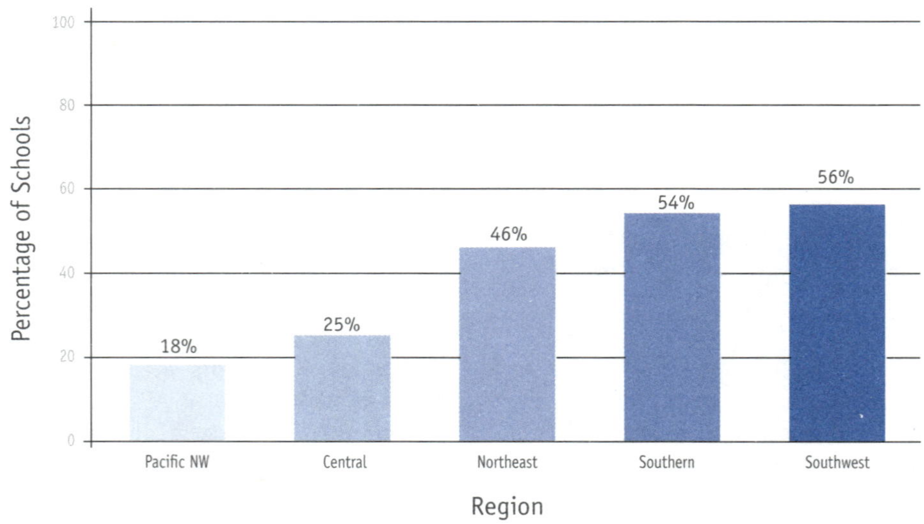

Figure 11. Advanced Placement Language Classes in High Schools (by Region) (2008).

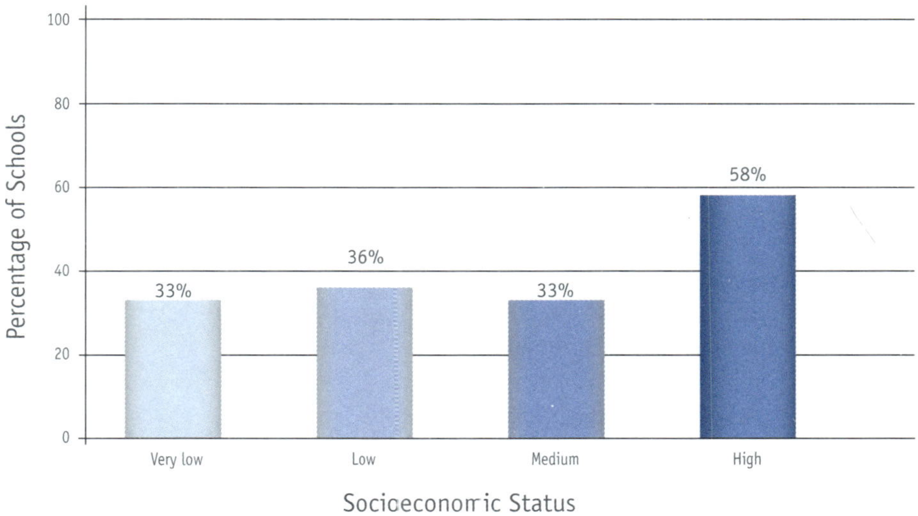

Figure 12. Advanced Placement Language Classes in Public High Schools (by Socioeconomic Status) (2008).

Note. Very low SES = ≥70% of students eligible for free or reduced-price lunch; low SES school = 40%–60% eligible; medium SES school = 20%–39% eligible; high SES school = <20% eligible.

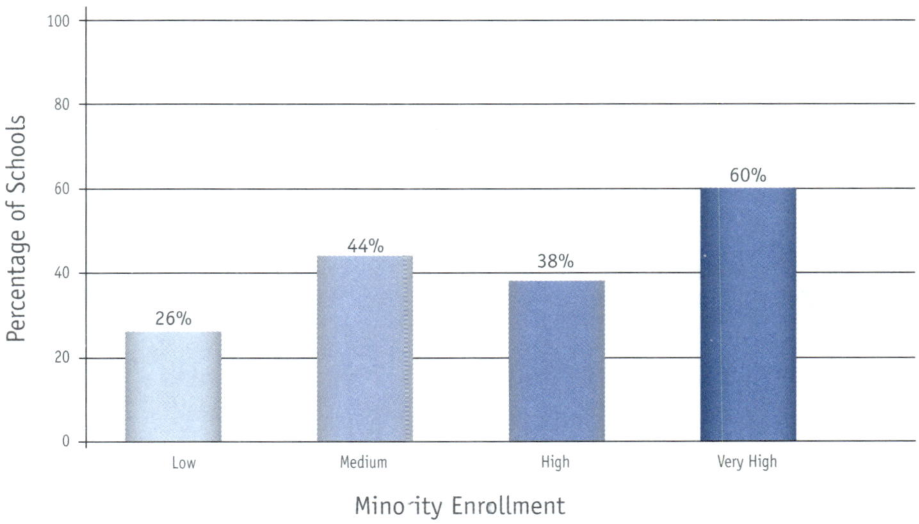

Figure 13. Advanced Placement Language Classes in High Schools (by Minority Enrollment) (2008).

Note. Low = <10% of minority student enrollment; medium = 10%–29% minority enrollment; high =30%–49% minority enrollment; very high = ≥50% minority enrollment.

the subjects taught in those schools varied considerably (Table 24).

In 2008, as in 1997, exploratory language classes were more prevalent in middle schools than in high schools: 45% of middle schools offered languages compared to 5% of high schools. (See Table 25 for breakdown by language.) Neither school size nor students' socioeconomic status was a factor in whether middle schools offered exploratory classes; however, schools with a low minority enrollment were more likely to offer exploratory classes than schools with a high minority enrollment. At the same time, 91% of middle schools offering foreign languages offered standard language classes (listening, speaking, reading, writing, and culture).

Table 24. Subjects Taught in Foreign Languages in Secondary Schools (2008)

Subjects taught in languages other than English	Languages used as medium of instruction
History/World history	French
Literature	German
Math/Algebra	Spanish
Physical education	
Science	
Social studies	
Theology	
World geography	

Distance learning classes were more likely to be offered by small schools, rural schools, and schools with low minority enrollment. IB courses, which were not included as an option in previous surveys, were offered by 3% of middle schools and 3% of high schools. They were more likely to be offered by urban and suburban schools, larger schools, and schools located in the Southern conference region. Schools also reported foreign language classes taken at nearby community colleges or university extension programs for college credit. More private schools than public schools reported offering literature classes, conversation classes, and honors/accelerated classes.

Grade and Course Levels and Amount of Instruction per Week

Elementary Schools

Public elementary schools with language programs offered language instruction fairly consistently across grade levels from Grades 1 through 5 (Table 26). They offered languages somewhat less often in kindergarten. The data presented here are from public elementary schools that taught the three most commonly offered languages: Spanish, French, and Chinese.

Table 25. Exploratory Language Classes Offered by Secondary Schools (1997, 2008)

	1997					2008				
	Publ. (%)	Priv. (%)	M.S. (%)	High (%)	Total (%)	Publ. (%)	Priv. (%)	M.S. (%)	High (%)	Total (%)
Spanish	21	13	45	3	20	13	7	28	5	11
French	14	8	30	2	13	6	4	16	1	5
General exploratory[a]	2	3	3	2	2			2	0.1	1
Japanese	2	0.1	4	0.4	2	0.9	0.6	2	0.4	0.9
German	6	1	11	1	5	0.9	0.7	3	0.1	0.8
Latin	2	2	5	0.3	2			0.8	0.4	0.6
Chinese	–	–	–	–	0.1			–	0.3	0.2

Note. In 1997, eight languages that were taught in exploratory classes at 0.4% or fewer schools with language programs did not appear in the 2008 survey: American Sign Language, Arabic, Hawaiian, Italian, Ojibwa, Portuguese, Russian, and Swahili. High = High School; M.S. = Middle School; Priv. = Private; Publ. = Public. Because some schools offered exploratory courses in more than one language, the sum of the percentages of all languages is greater than the total percentage of schools offering exploratory classes (45% M.S. and 5% H.S.). A dash (–) indicates that the *n* was too small to calculate percentage.

[a]This category includes such offerings as Introduction to Language(s), Exploratory Language, World Language(s), Exploring (New) Languages, Awareness of Language, and various combinations of languages.

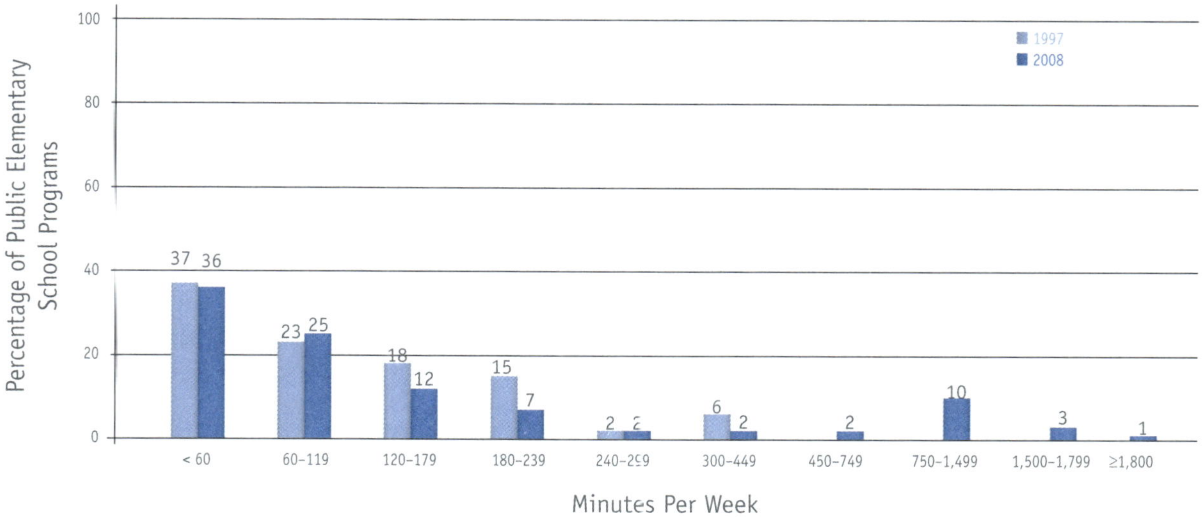

Figure 14. Average Minutes Per Week of Instruction in Public Elementary School Language Programs (1997, 2008)

Note. For 1997, the category 300–449 minutes was labeled 300+ minutes, thus was the highest possible category.

Table 26. Elementary School Language Instruction (by Grade Level) (2008)

GRADE	Public elementary schools with language programs (%)
K	61
1	74
2	75
3	76
4	77
5	74

The number of minutes per week of instruction is shown in Figure 14. These data were based on the number of language programs rather than the number of schools, because schools may offer more than one language program with differing minutes of instruction. Although 14% of programs (last three bars in Figure 14) provided 750 minutes or more of instruction per week, the majority (61%; first two 2008 bars in Figure 14) provided less than 120 minutes per week, with 36% of programs providing less than 60 minutes per week. These numbers were largely unchanged from 1997. While the percentage of language programs that offered more than 300 minutes of instruction per week increased substantially between 1997 and 2008, the number of programs that offered 120–180 minutes or 180–240 minutes per week decreased.

Secondary Schools

Secondary schools with foreign language programs reported offering a variety of levels of instruction (Table 27). A majority of high schools offering the top four languages (Spanish, French, German, and Latin) offered courses from level 1 to level 4. Level 4 Spanish was offered by a smaller percentage of schools than level 4 French, German, and Latin. A possible explanation is that many schools offer AP Spanish instead of the level 4 course, followed by AP Spanish literature instead of level 5. Levels 2 and higher were offered primarily in high schools. The majority of middle schools offered level 1, with some offering more advanced levels. The average amount of weekly class time in secondary schools in the top four languages was down slightly from 1997, to under 5 hours.

Table 27. Course Levels in Secondary Schools Offering Spanish, French, German, and/or Latin (2008)

	Middle (%)	High (%)	Total (%)
Level 1			
Spanish	99	99	99
French	100	95	96
German	92	95	95
Latin	100	98	99
Level 2			
Spanish	42	97	83
French	42	97	85
German	38	93	83
Latin	71	87	86
Level 3			
Spanish	8	75	55
French	9	83	68
German	8	76	64
Latin	49	77	75
Level 4			
Spanish	1	55	41
French	1	69	54
German	0	63	52
Latin	25	67	64
Level 5			
Spanish	0	23	17
French	0	32	25
German	0	28	23
Latin	0	21	20
Level 6			
Spanish	0	6	5
French	0	8	6
German	0	4	3
Latin	0	5	5

Table 28. Elementary Schools With Foreign Language Classes That Last for the Entire School Year (1997, 2008)

	1997 (%)	2008 (%)
Public	70	90
Private	85	95
Total	77	93

Table 29. Elementary Schools With Foreign Language Classes That Last for Less Than the Entire School Year (2008)

	Public (%)	Private (%)	Total (%)
1–5 weeks	2	6	4
6–10 weeks	22	21	22
11–15 weeks	21	22	21
More than 15 weeks	55	52	54

Note. Totals may equal more than 100% due to rounding.

Table 30. Secondary Schools With Foreign Language Classes That Last for the Entire School Year (1997, 2008)

	1997 (%)	2008 (%)
Public	72	80
Private	90	94
Middle school	51	70
High school	87	87
Total	74	83

Scheduling

Elementary Schools

In 2008, the vast majority (93%) of foreign language classes offered at elementary schools lasted the entire school year. This represented an increase from 1997 (Table 28). There was no variation across the various stratification factors (e.g., type of school, metro status, school size). Among foreign language classes that did not last the entire school year, 96% lasted at least 6 weeks and 54% lasted more than 15 weeks (Table 29).

Secondary Schools

In 2008, most of the foreign language classes offered at secondary schools lasted the entire school year. Although language classes at private schools were more likely to last the entire year than those at public schools, both types of schools showed an increase in the percentage of year-long classes since 1997 (Table 30). As in 1997, middle schools were less likely to offer year-long classes than high schools, but the overall increase in year-long classes at the secondary level

Table 31. Secondary Schools With Foreign Language Classes That Last Less Than a Year (2008)

	Public (%)	Private (%)	Total (%)
1–5 weeks	2	3	2
6–10 weeks	26	32	27
11–15 weeks	15	17	15
More than 15 weeks	57	48	56

Note. Totals may equal more than 100% due to rounding.

was due largely to the increase at the middle-school level. Almost all secondary school language classes that did not last the entire school year lasted at least 6 weeks, and more than half lasted more than 15 weeks (Table 31).

Discussion

While the teaching of Spanish, the most commonly taught language, increased significantly at the elementary level and remained stable at the secondary level, the teaching of French and German saw significant declines at both levels. In a positive trend, some of the less commonly taught languages were offered at more schools in 2008 than in 1997. The percentage of schools offering Chinese and Arabic, although still low, increased at both the elementary and secondary levels. Russian and Japanese, however, decreased at both levels. The ups and downs in the teaching of various world languages appear to be a response to major world events (e.g., Russian was more popular in the 1980s, Japanese in the 1990s, Chinese and Arabic in the 2000s). Many language education leaders are distressed at the zero-sum-game aspect of language education, where the increase in enrollment in one language results in a decrease in enrollment in other languages (Board Members of the Joint National Committee on Languages, personal communication, February 27, 2009).

One interesting option that has been proposed for the elementary school level, because of the shortage of teachers and resources in most languages, is to offer only one language to all elementary school students in a school district. This would provide them with a strong base in language learning. Then, in middle school and high school, students would have the option of continuing the original language and/or switching to or adding one or more other languages (R. Kline, personal communication, February 27, 2009). This is a variation of a model that is used in Europe, where most primary schools offer English instruction, with instruction in other languages added in later grades (Education, Audiovisual & Culture Executive Agency, 2008).

U.S. federal agencies have stated that the advantages of developing advanced language proficiency and cultural knowledge in any language at a young age are far more important than the choice of the language taught. "Even if it turns out that the language and culture learned . . . [are] extraneous to a particular government position, it has been our experience that individuals who have learned one foreign language well tend to learn another well also, even if it is not in the same language family" (Eddy, 1998, pp. 91-92). This presents a strong case for providing language instruction in any language to elementary school children and then offering them options as they move through secondary school and on to college.

An important question is the level of language proficiency being attained by elementary school students. Exploratory programs, by definition, do not provide instruction that will lead to any level of proficiency, yet they made up 44% of the elementary programs offered. Only immersion programs (partial, total, and two-way) consistently provide instruction that allows students to attain a high level of proficiency, but they made up only 6% of elementary language programs. With language focus programs, the amount of instructional time varies widely; it is not known what percentage of these programs provided enough instructional time for students to develop proficiency. Looking at all program types combined, survey results showed that the majority of schools offered language instruction for less than 120 minutes per week, with more than one third of those offering instruction for less than 60 minutes per week. The ACTFL Performance Guidelines for K-12 Learners (Swender & Duncan, 1998) report that student outcomes correlate with time in program and recommend that elementary school students be offered programs that meet "3–5 days per week for no less than 30–40 minutes per class." Clearly, a large number of elementary schools in 2008 were not offering the recommended amount of instruction for students to attain proficiency.

At the secondary school level, almost all programs reported offering traditional language classes that included listening, speaking, reading, writing, and culture. Although there was an increase in the percentage of schools offering Advanced Placement, International Baccalaureate, and classes for heritage language speakers, suggesting a trend toward more advanced classes, the numbers were still low. A positive finding was that many schools with large minority populations were offering AP language classes. In addition, the College Board (2009) reports that heritage language speakers represent a large proportion of AP test takers of Chinese language, Spanish language, and Spanish literature. On the down side, there was still a disparity in access to AP classes, with rural, small, and low SES schools and schools in certain regions of the country less likely to offer AP language classes. Moreover, Spanish AP test results for 2008 show that the majority of students who received most of their foreign language training in U.S. schools did not score high enough on the exam to receive college credit (i.e., a score of at least 3 on a scale of 1 to 5) (College Board, 2009).

CHAPTER 5: CURRICULUM AND INSTRUCTION

This chapter provides results on the use of a foreign language curriculum or guidelines, the types of instructional materials and assessment strategies used, teachers' use of the foreign language in the classroom, and various models of program articulation. These results provide key information on what is taking place in language classrooms across the country and on the extent to which schools and districts plan for articulated instruction from one school level to the next. Results for each section are presented first for elementary schools, then for secondary schools.

Curriculum or Guidelines

Elementary Schools

More than three quarters of elementary schools teaching foreign languages reported having an established and written foreign language curriculum or set of guidelines for their program (Figure 15). There was a gradual increase in the percentage of schools using curricula over the three survey periods, from 64% in 1987 to 70% in 1997 to 78% in 2008.

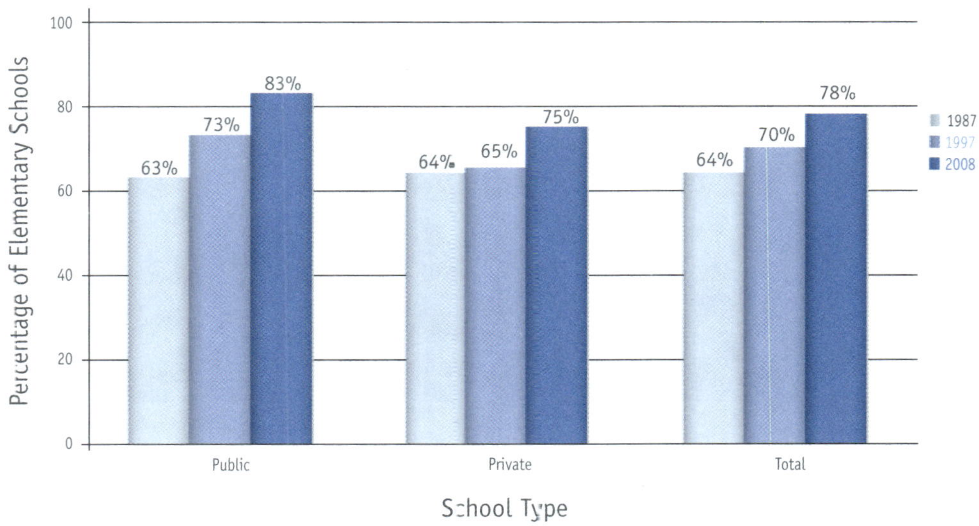

Figure 15. Foreign Language Curriculum or Guidelines in Elementary Schools (by School Type) (1987, 1997, 2008).

Note. There were no statistically significant differences between 1987 and 1997. No statistical tests were conducted on 2008 data.

In 2008, the existence of a foreign language curriculum or set of guidelines varied according to school type and metro status. Among all schools with foreign language programs, more public than private schools reported having a foreign language curriculum or guidelines. Among public elementary schools, suburban schools (91%) more frequently had a foreign language curriculum than urban (83%) or rural (73%) schools. Among private elementary schools, rural (79%) and suburban (78%) schools more frequently had a foreign language curriculum than urban (69%) schools.

Secondary Schools

The vast majority of secondary schools reported having an established and written foreign language curriculum or set of guidelines. This percentage stayed fairly steady over the three survey periods (Figure 16).

In 2008, the existence of a foreign language curriculum or set of guidelines varied according to metro status, school size, and minority enrollment. Among public secondary schools, suburban schools (94%) were more likely to have a foreign language curriculum than urban (86%) or rural (80%) schools. Among private secondary schools, urban schools (93%) were more likely to have a foreign language curriculum than rural (78%) or suburban (76%) schools. Overall, medium, large, and very large schools (90%, 96%, 91%) were more likely than small schools (74%) to have language curricula. Schools with higher minority enrollments were more likely to have a written foreign language curriculum than schools with a low minority enrollment (88% of schools with medium, high, or very high minority enrollment vs. 80% of schools with low minority enrollment). The existence of a foreign language curriculum was fairly consistent across geographic regions, with the majority of schools in all regions reporting having a foreign language curriculum.

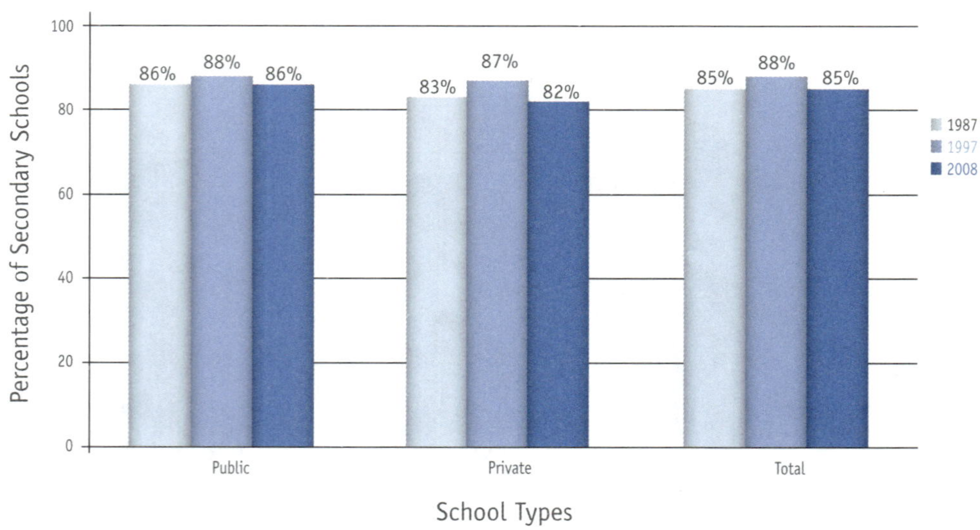

Figure 16. Foreign Language Curriculum or Guidelines in Secondary Schools (by School Type) (1987, 1997, 2008).

Note. There were no statistically significant differences between 1987 and 1997. No statistical tests were conducted on 2008 data.

Instructional Materials

Elementary Schools

In 2008, the three most popular types of materials for teaching foreign languages at the elementary level were literature from the target culture (e.g., stories, books, songs, poems/rhymes), visual-tactile materials (e.g., puppets, posters, pictures, flash cards, games, puzzles), and teacher-made materials category (Table 32). Whereas the use of teacher-made materials category stayed at about the same level from 1997 to 2008, the use of literature from the target culture increased to a statistically significant degree. Visual/tactile materials were not listed as a separate category in 1997 but were frequently mentioned under the Teacher-made materials category.

The next most commonly used materials were audiovisual media (e.g., films, videotapes, DVDs, CDs, audiotapes); authentic materials from the target culture, known as realia (e.g., menus, magazines, advertisements, newspapers, bus tickets); and commercially published textbooks and workbooks. The use of various technology-based materials increased to a statistically significant degree from 1997 to 2008. In 2008, Internet resources (e.g., World Wide Web, online activities, virtual tours, electronic mail, discussion lists, chats, blogs, wikis, podcasts) were used in foreign language instruction by 70% of elementary schools, more than triple the percentage in 1997. The use of computer-assisted instructional materials (e.g., computer software programs, CD-ROMs) increased from 41% to 59%, and the use of other instructional technologies (e.g., satellite broadcasts, interactive television, video conferencing) increased from 10% to 23%. Finally, 37% of schools reported using other types of instructional materials and resources, such as international pen pals, native speakers and people from the community, television programs, and college foreign language students.

There were a few variations according to school type, metro status, and school size. Public elementary schools reported using more Internet resources, audiovisual media, and other technology than private schools, while private schools were more likely than public schools to report using commercially published textbooks. Rural schools were less likely than urban and suburban schools to use authentic materials from the target culture or commercially published textbooks, but they were more likely to use materials in the Other category.

Table 32. Instructional Materials Used by Elementary School Foreign Language Programs (by School Type) (1997, 2008)

	1997			2008		
	Public (%)	Private (%)	Total (%)	Public (%)	Private (%)	Total (%)
Literature from the target culture	73	64	69[a]	99	95	96[a]
Visual/tactile materials	–	–	–	98	95	96
Teacher-made materials	93	96	94	99	93	95
Audiovisual media	95	93	94	94	88	90
Authentic materials from target culture	73	6	74	82	81	81
Commercially published textbooks/ workbooks	78	94	85	70	86	79
Internet resources	21	17	19[a]	84	67	70[a]
Computer-assisted instructional materials	43	39	41[a]	61	58	59[a]
Other technology	15	3	10[a]	27	20	23[a]
Other materials	21	12	17[a]	51	26	37[a]

Note. Dash (–) = data not collected in 1997.

[a] Difference between 1997 and 2008 was statistically significant.

Secondary Schools

The six most commonly used instructional materials in secondary school language programs were literature from the target culture (which showed a statistically significant increase from 1997), commercially published textbooks/workbooks, teacher-made materials, audio visual materials, visual/tactile materials, and authentic materials from the target culture (Table 33). The use of three categories of materials increased to a statistically significant degree from 1997 to 2008: Internet resources, computer-assisted materials, and other instructional technology. The use of other instructional materials and resources (e.g., field trips, pen pals, native-speaker guests, Total Physical Response activities, interactive white boards, and language laboratories) also increased.

There were some notable variations across school type and school level. Public secondary schools were more likely than private secondary schools to use Internet resources and visual/tactile materials. The difference between middle schools and high schools that reported using authentic literature and realia in 1997 had disappeared by 2008: 98% of both middle schools and high schools reported using authentic literature; 93% of middle schools and 92% of high schools reported using realia.

Proficiency Assessment

Elementary Schools

Elementary school respondents reported using a wide range of strategies to assess students' language proficiency (Figure 17). The three most frequently used strategies[17] focused on comprehension (both listening and reading) and oral proficiency: asking students to use illustrations to indicate understanding, having students explain in English what they heard or read in the target language, and having students engage in oral language activities, such as short interviews or interpersonal exchanges in the target language. These three strategies were not included in the 1997 survey. The only types of assessment that showed a marked change from 1997 were translation exercises, which increased from 58% to 70%, probably due at least in part to an increase in Latin instruction, and self-assessment by students, which increased from 31% to 51%.

Sixty respondents added written comments about assessment, many of which reinforced the subcategories already selected. Almost half listed the name of a specific standardized assessment used, while others mentioned data-gathering strategies, such as teacher

[17] These three assessment types were included for the first time in 2008 at the suggestion of project advisors.

Table 33. Instructional Materials Used by Secondary School Foreign Language Programs (by School Type) (1997, 2008)

	1997			2008		
	Public (%)	Private (%)	Total (%)	Public (%)	Private (%)	Total (%)
Literature from the target culture	83	84	83[a]	99	97	98[a]
Commercially published textbooks/workbooks	98	100	98	98	97	98
Teacher-made materials	96	91	95	99	93	98
Audiovisual media	99	93	99	98	95	97
Visual/tactile materials	–	–	–	98	89	96
Authentic materials from target culture	93	89	92	94	89	92
Internet resources	39	41	39[a]	91	76	87[a]
Computer-assisted instructional materials	52	53	52[a]	80	79	80[a]
Other technology	31	21	30[a]	38	32	37[a]
Other materials	21	12	17[a]	45	69	52[a]

Note. Dash (–) = data not collected in 1997.

[a] Difference between 1997 and 2008 was statistically significant.

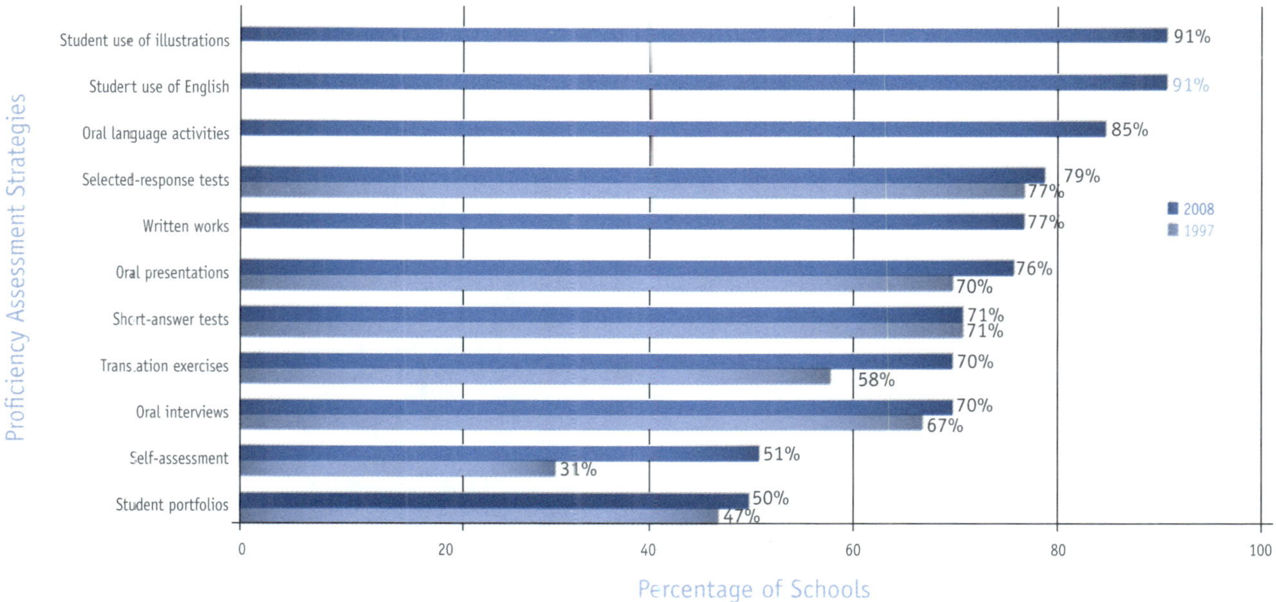

Figure 17. Language Proficiency Assessment Strategies Used by Elementary Schools (1997, 2008).

Note. Missing responses indicate the responses were not an option in the 1997 survey.

observations, or specific projects in which language and cultural skills were assessed, such as setting up a market place for oral language practice in the classroom.

The most apparent difference between public and private schools was that public schools used more student self-assessment (56% vs. 47%) while private schools used more short-answer tests (74% vs. 66%) and translation exercises (80% vs. 55%). The difference in the use of translation exercises is most likely the result of Latin being taught in more private than public elementary schools.

Secondary Schools

In 2008, the most widely used types of assessment at the secondary level were selected-response tests, short-answer tests, and written works such as essays and reports (Figure 18). Almost as widely employed were assessments of comprehension and oral proficiency, including student use of English, student use of illustrations, oral language activities, and oral presentations. The use of oral proficiency interviews, student self-assessment, and student portfolios increased substantially from 1997 to 2008. The only notable differences between middle schools and high schools were in the use of standardized tests (53% of high schools vs. 33% of middle schools) and in the use of other assessments (63% of high schools vs. 42% of middle schools). Many of the assessments that were mentioned by respondents under Other overlapped with the list of assessment items provided in the questionnaire, particularly standardized exams. Respondents also mentioned using exams that were created for college credit, SAT subject tests (for high school students), the production of podcasts, and Web-based activities.

The most apparent difference between public and private secondary schools was that public schools used more oral language activities (97% vs. 90%) and student self-assessment (75% vs. 53%). There were notable differences among urban, suburban, and rural schools. Urban (74%) and suburban (61%) schools were more likely to use standardized exams than rural schools (35%). The same pattern emerged with respect to socioeconomic status: The higher the SES, the more likely the school was to use standardized tests. Suburban schools were most likely to use oral proficiency interviews (95% vs. urban 89% and rural 82%) and student self-assessment (74% vs. 67% for both urban and rural schools), while urban schools were more likely to use portfolios (66% vs. suburban 60% and rural 54%).

Teacher Language Use in the Classroom

In 2008, both elementary and secondary school respondents were asked to what extent teachers used the foreign language in the classroom.[18] During the previous survey periods, this question was asked only of the secondary schools.

[18] a) It should be noted that empirical studies have shown that many teachers vastly overestimate the amount of time that is spent in the target language (Wilkerson, 2008). The data nevertheless provide important insights about what teachers and principals think should be the goal with respect to foreign language use in the classroom.

b) For schools that had more than one program type, respondents were asked to indicate foreign language use in the language classes that aim for the highest proficiency.

c) Responses for immersion programs were not included in these tabulations because these programs, by definition, use the target language for almost 100% of the language immersion classes.

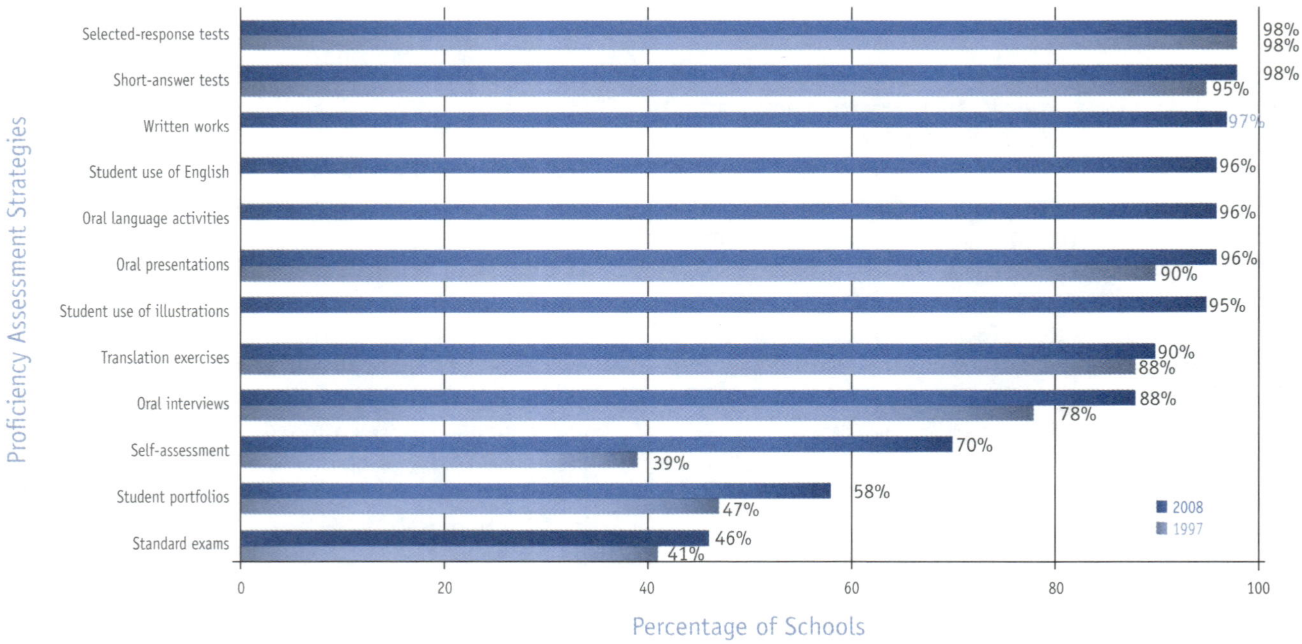

Figure 18. Language Proficiency Assessment Strategies Used by Secondary Schools (1997, 2008).

Note. Missing responses indicate the responses were not an option in the 1997 survey.

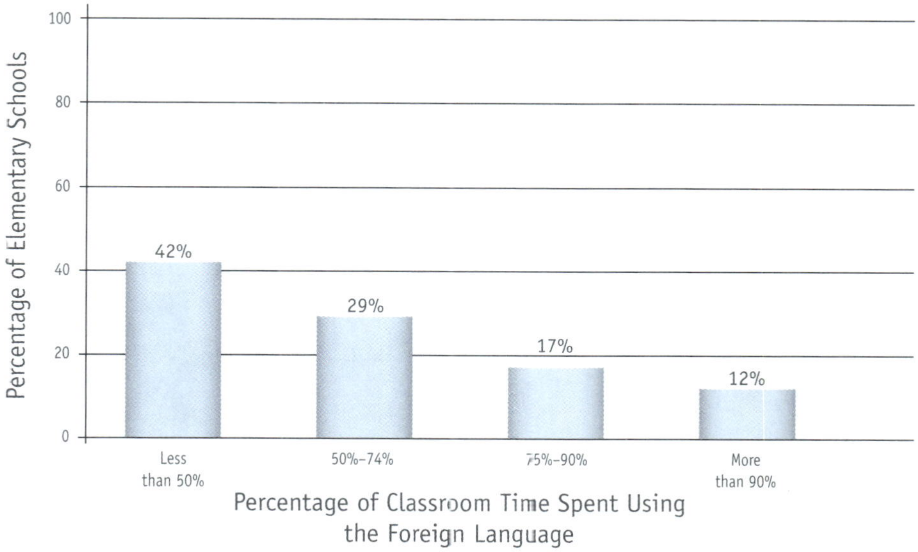

Figure 19. Elementary Teachers' Use of the Foreign Language in Non-Immersion Foreign Language Classes (2008).

Elementary Schools

In 2008, 42% of elementary schools with language focus or exploratory language programs reported that their teachers used the foreign language in class less than half the time; only 12% said that their teachers used the foreign language more than 90% of the time (Figure 19). The only difference of note between public and private schools was that more public than private schools (17% vs. 9%) reported teachers using the foreign language in class more than 90% of the time. There were some differences among regions. The Northeast had the highest percentage of schools reporting teacher use of the foreign language more than 90% of the time and the lowest percentage reporting foreign language use less than 50% of the time. No clear patterns emerged among any of the other variables.

Secondary Schools

Between 1997 and 2008, there was a statistically significant increase in the percentage of secondary schools reporting that their language teachers used the foreign language in class at least 75% of the time and a significant decrease in the percentage of schools reporting foreign language use less than 50% of the time. In 2008, 36% of schools reported that their teachers used the foreign language in class at least 75% of the time; 21% reported using it less than 50% of the time (Figure 20).

In 2008, there was little variation in reported use of the foreign language by school level (middle vs. high school), type of school (public or private), minority enrollment, or socioeconomic status. However, there was some variation according to metro status, school size, and conference region. Rural schools were less likely than urban or suburban schools, and smaller schools were less likely than larger schools, to report high foreign language use. Schools in the Northeast and Southwest conference regions reported higher foreign language use than schools in the other regions.

A comparison of teachers' use of the target language at the three school levels revealed that among all

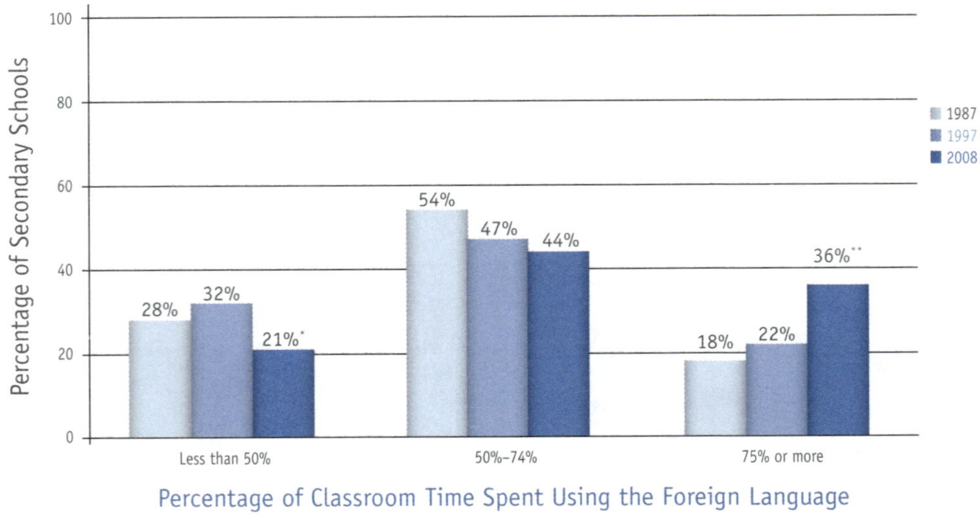

Figure 20. Secondary Teachers' Use of the Foreign Language in the Classroom (1987, 1997, 2008).

Note. For 2008, the categories *75%–90% of the time* and *more than 90% of the time* were combined to allow comparison with 1987 and 1997 data. Totals may equal more than 100% due to rounding.
* Significant decrease from 1997 to 2008.
** Significant increase from 1997 to 2008.

schools, elementary teachers used the target language less than middle school and high school teachers (Figure 21).

Program Articulation

Elementary Schools

As in the two previous surveys, elementary school respondents in 2008 indicated that articulation (i.e., sequencing of instruction in which each level builds on the previous level) to ensure continuity in foreign language study from one level of schooling to the next was a major challenge. Half of all respondents (50%), up from 45% in 1997, reported that instruction for their language students was not articulated from one level to the next. Most of these respondents (30% of all respondents) indicated that students who had studied a foreign language in elementary school were placed in level 1 classes in middle school, along with students who had had no prior instruction in the language. A smaller percentage (12% of all respondents) indicated that their elementary school foreign language students were placed in exploratory language classes in middle school, and 8% noted that the foreign languages taught in their elementary schools were not offered at the middle schools (Figure 22).

Only 39% of elementary schools reported that their districts or schools had some type of articulation in place. They reported using three types of articulation: middle school classes specifically designed to provide continuity from students' language study in elementary school, advanced language classes that were not specifically designed to reflect students' prior language study, and subject matter courses taught in the foreign language. No major variation was found across the various stratification factors.

Eleven percent of respondents marked the Other category for articulation (meaning that none of the options listed on the questionnaire applied to their

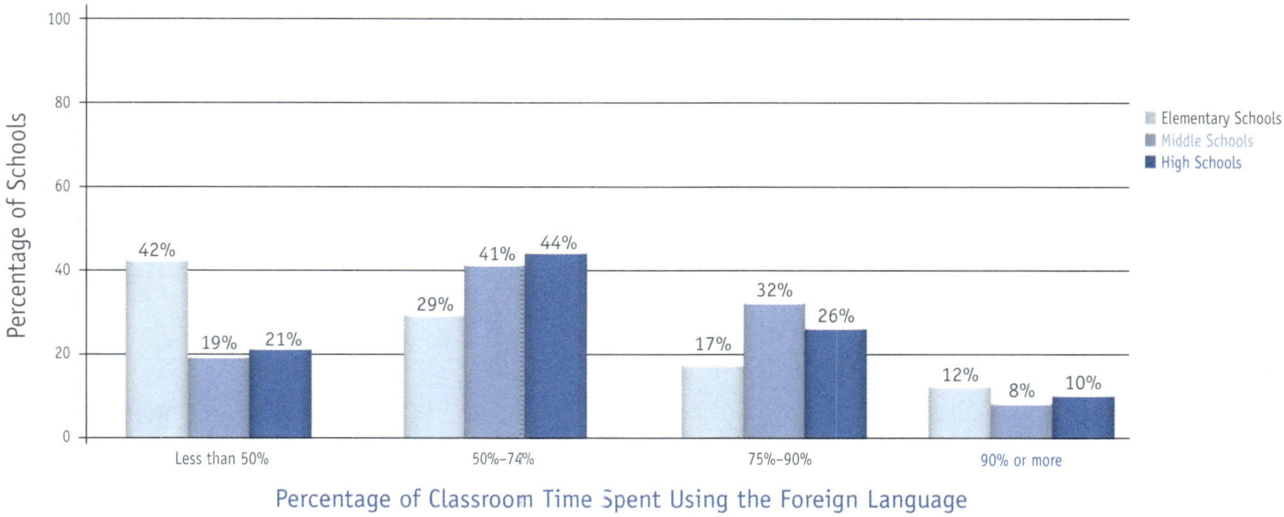

Figure 21. Teachers' Use of the Foreign Language in the Classroom (by School Level) (2008).

situation). Several of these respondents said they did not know in what language classes their students continued in middle school or whether they continued their language study at all. Others reported that their elementary language program had not existed long enough for them to have graduated any students, but some of them said they were involved in planning for articulation. One public school respondent commented, "Our first group is rolling up into middle school for fall '08. We are in collaborative planning currently." Other respondents reported using placement tests, student choice, or miscellaneous options when placing students into language classes in secondary school.

Secondary Schools

About one quarter of high school respondents reported that their incoming students had not received foreign language instruction during their middle school years. Respondents whose incoming students had studied foreign languages previously reported a variety of class offerings for these students. Many schools designed sequencing strategies to ensure that students' language instruction in high school built on what they had learned in middle school (Figure 23).

Of the high schools whose students had had prior language experience, 55% reported that those students were placed in advanced classes specifically designed to provide continuity from their prior language study—a noticeable increase from 24% in 1997. Only 3% of high schools in 2008 reported placing students in advanced classes that were not necessarily a continuation of their prior language study, a clear decrease from 1997. Only 1% reported the availability of subject matter courses taught in the foreign language. In 30% of high schools, incoming students with prior language instruction were placed in level 1 classes with students who did not have prior foreign language experience; this is a decrease from 1997. A small percentage were placed in exploratory language classes. Of the respondents who marked Other, 20 provided optional comments (7 from public schools, 13 from private). Twelve of the private

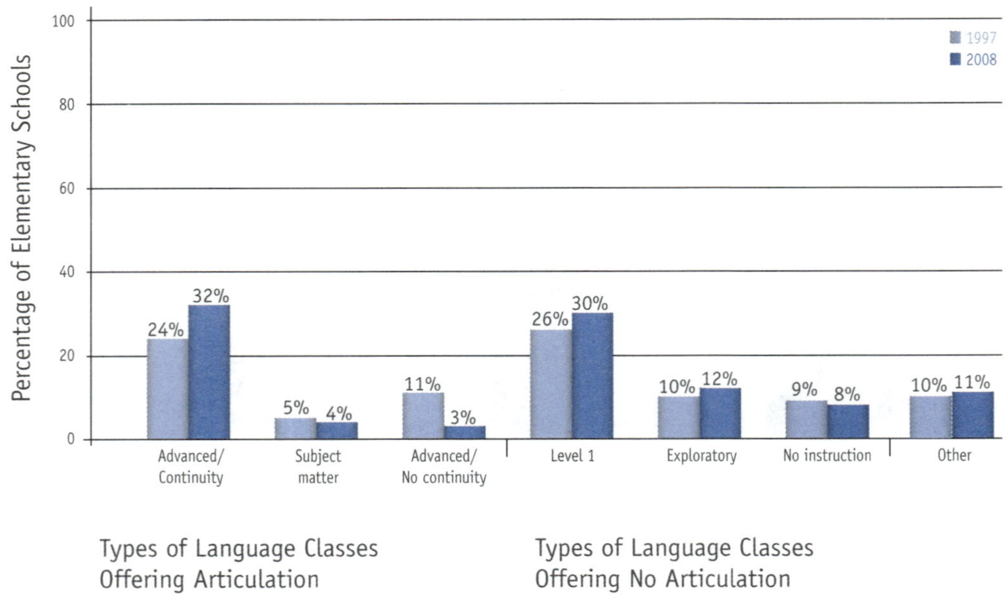

Figure 22. Patterns for Articulation From Elementary to Middle School Language Study (1997,2008).

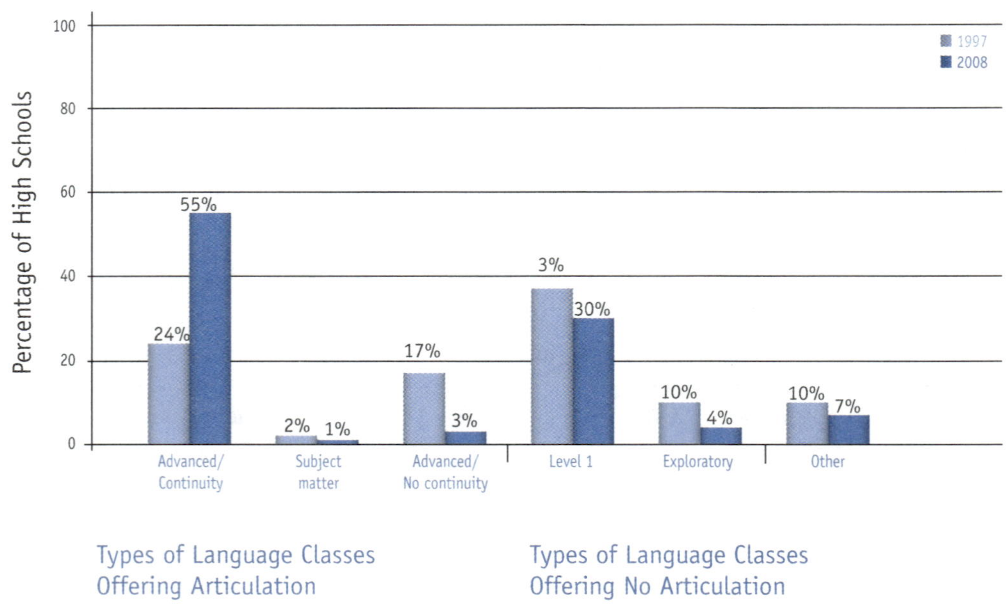

Figure 23. Patterns for Articulation From Middle School to High School Language Study (1997, 2008).

school respondents who offered comments reported that students with prior foreign language study were given a placement test; the other private school respondent reported that students were placed according to their individual situation. All of the comments from public school respondents indicated that students were either given placement tests or placed in the appropriate high school class based on their success in middle school foreign language classes.

Discussion

Results revealed some positive trends in curriculum and instruction over the past decade. As was true in both previous surveys, the vast majority of secondary schools reported having an established foreign language curriculum. At the elementary school level, there was a gradual increase over 20 years in the percentage of schools reporting an established and written foreign language curriculum, from 64% in 1987 to 78% in 2008. This seems to indicate that elementary schools have given more status to their language programs and have moved away from the earlier, informal programs that were not standards based or proficiency oriented.

The most noticeable change in the use of instructional materials over the past decade was in the use of technology-based materials. The use of Internet resources tripled at the elementary level and doubled at the secondary level, and the use of both computer-assisted instructional materials and other instructional technology increased significantly at both levels. These changes were no doubt a result of the wider availability of computers in schools compared to a decade ago and of advances in computer technology that provide new opportunities for interactivity to enhance language learning. The disparity between public and private schools in the use of some technologies was evident (both elementary and secondary public schools used more technology) as was the disparity between small schools and large schools (larger secondary schools used more technology).

A positive change seen at both the elementary and secondary levels was the increased use of literature from the target culture. This change may reflect teachers' increasing awareness of authentic materials from the countries where the target language is spoken. It may also reflect an increased focus on implementing the national standards for foreign language instruction, especially the standards dealing with connections to additional bodies of knowledge that are sometimes unavailable to monolingual English speakers and those that address comparisons and contrasts with other world views.

Another positive trend at both levels of instruction was an increase in the use of student self-assessments, in which students take an active role in monitoring their language development. (See National Capital Language Resource Center, n.d., for information on the benefits of self-assessment in language learning using portfolios.) A possible contributing factor to this increase is the introduction in 2003 of the user-friendly LinguaFolio, a portfolio assessment instrument designed to help individual learners establish their own goals for language learning and document their progress toward greater proficiency (National Council of State Supervisors for Languages, 2009). One indication of the growing use of LinguaFolio is the number of states involved in pilot testing (Georgia, Kentucky, North Carolina, South Carolina, and Virginia; LinguaFolio, n.d.); another is the number of presentations on its use at foreign language conventions in recent years.

The 2008 survey also revealed an increase by both elementary and secondary schools in the use of proficiency-oriented assessments, including oral presentations, oral interviews, and student portfolios. As more schools align their curricula with the national standards, it is anticipated that teachers will incorporate additional performance-based assessments into their teaching in order to more accurately assess the proficiency of their students.

At the elementary school level, the three most common strategies for assessing language proficiency focused on listening and reading comprehension and oral proficiency. In contrast, the most commonly used assessment types at the secondary level were the more traditional selected-response and short-answer tests, which tend to include traditional discrete-point or grammar-based questions. Although it is difficult to generalize from these results, assessment methods often mirror teaching techniques, which may mean that instructional practices at the secondary level are more traditional (focusing more on grammar) than those at the elementary level.

It is a positive sign that in 2008, secondary school teachers were using the target language in the classroom more than they did a decade ago, but most were not speaking in the target language all the time. Experts in language education have long realized that successful language learning requires substantial exposure to the target language, referred to as "comprehensible input" (Krashen, 1985). In the classroom, this means that the target language has to "become the medium as well as the object of instruction" (Ellis, 2008). Teachers are therefore urged to use the target language consistently and extensively from the very first day of instruction and for all classroom activities and tasks (Curtain & Dahlberg, 2004).

It is possible, however, that some teachers do not speak the language they teach well enough to conduct their classes solely through that language. Teachers' age and background may also influence their use of the language in class. Teachers who entered the profession prior to the move from grammar-based instruction to teaching for proficiency in the 1980s may not be aware of the value of speaking the target language as much as possible in the classroom. Those who began teaching before 1996, when the national standards were first published and made widely available, or even before 2002, when the standards for the preparation of foreign language teachers were completed, might be unaware of the changes in focus in language teaching, especially if they do not participate regularly in subject-specific professional development, attend language teacher conferences, or read academic journals in their field. The measure of most teachers' use of the target language is directly related to when they received their teacher preparation and how much they have incorporated updated philosophies of language teaching (e.g., teaching for proficiency, adhering to common standards) into their own instruction (M. H. Rosenbusch, personal communication, August 28, 2009).

An area of concern is the lack of articulation between school levels reported by 50% of elementary schools and 34% of high schools. Appropriate program articulation is a critical factor in the development of high levels of language proficiency (National Standards in Foreign Language Education Project, 2006). One positive sign was that in 2008, more high schools than in the past reported placing students with prior language experience in advanced classes specifically designed to provide continuity from their previous language study. But for long-sequence foreign language programs to be possible, much more collaboration and coordination will be needed between elementary and secondary schools.

CHAPTER 6: FOREIGN LANGUAGE TEACHERS

This chapter provides results on the number of foreign language teachers at schools, teacher certification and professional development, and language teacher shortages and hiring practices. These results provide useful information on the status of language teachers in public and private schools and ways some schools are addressing a teacher shortage. Results for each section are presented first for elementary schools, then for secondary schools.

Number of Teachers

Elementary Schools

Elementary schools offering foreign language instruction had slightly more foreign language teachers on staff in 2008 than in 1997. In 2008, only 4% of elementary schools offering foreign language instruction reported having no foreign language teacher, compared to 11% in 1997.[19] Just over half of the elementary schools teaching foreign languages in 2008 had one full- or part-time foreign language teacher, a slight decrease from 1997, while the percentage of schools with two language teachers increased from 12% to 20% (Table 34). Private schools were more likely than public schools to have two to five teachers, whereas public schools were more likely than private schools to have more than six foreign language teachers.

Secondary Schools[20]

At the secondary level, 35% of schools with language programs had one full- or part-time foreign language teacher, up slightly from 1997 (Table 35). Public schools were slightly more likely than private schools to have only one or two foreign language teachers, whereas private schools were more likely to have three or more foreign language teachers. Rural schools were much more likely than urban or suburban schools to have only one foreign language teacher (52% vs. urban 23% and suburban 20%), most likely a reflection of their smaller student enrollment.

Table 34. Number of Foreign Language Teachers in Elementary Schools (by School Type) (1997, 2008)

	Public		Private		Total	
	1997 (%)	2008 (%)	1997 (%)	2008 (%)	1997 (%)	2008 (%)
None	14	5	7	3	11	4
One	52	51	55	52	53	51
Two	NA	15	NA	23	12	20
Three to five	NA	11	NA	18	15	14
Six to nine	NA	9	NA	3	6	6
Ten or more	NA	7	NA	1	3	5

Note. NA = data were not available.

[19] This is possible because elementary schools may offer foreign language instruction via satellite or video, facilitated by a regular classroom teacher.

[20] The number of language teachers per school is related to school size, especially at the secondary school level. However, data on the number of teachers are not available to be presented by school size.

Table 35. Number of Foreign Language Teachers in Secondary Schools (by School Type) (1997, 2008)

	Public		Private		Total	
	1997 (%)	2008 (%)	1997 (%)	2008 (%)	1997 (%)	2008 (%)
None	0	2	0	4	0	2
One	32	36	21	31	31	35
Two	NA	19	NA	16	21	18
Three to five	NA	24	NA	30	32	26
Six to nine	NA	14	NA	12	13	14
Ten or more	NA	5	NA	7	4	4

Note. Percentages do not equal 100% due to rounding. NA = data were not available.

Teacher Certification

For the 2008 survey question on teacher certification, respondents were asked to indicate the number of foreign language teachers in their school who had various certifications. Responses were tabulated in two ways. First, to provide information about the qualifications of the foreign language teaching force, the percentage of teachers holding each type of certification was calculated. Second, to allow comparisons between 1997 and 2008 data and to discern trends in language teacher certification, the percentage of schools with *at least one* teacher holding each type of certification was calculated. Several response categories were changed between the 1997 and 2008 surveys. Two categories (college students and volunteers) were collapsed into the category of noncertified teachers.

Elementary Schools

In 2008, elementary schools with foreign language programs reported that 76% of their language teachers had some type of teacher certification and 24% did not. Public school teachers were more likely than private school teachers to be certified (83% vs. 70%; Table 36).

For public schools, there was considerable variation by metro status, with more rural schools reporting that they had no teachers certified to teach foreign languages (Table 37). For example, 37% of rural public school language teachers were not certified compared to 13% of urban and 12% of suburban language teachers; 32% of rural public school language teachers were certified for elementary school teaching but not for foreign language teaching (vs. urban 15% and suburban 17%).

Table 36. Certifications of Elementary School Language Teachers (by School Type) (2008)

	Public (%)	Private (%)	Total (%)
Foreign language teaching at the elementary school level *and* for elementary school teaching	41	7	25
Foreign language teaching at the K–12 level	19	22	21
Foreign language teaching at the elementary school level	22	15	19
Elementary school teaching, but *not* specifically for foreign language	19	17	18
Foreign language teaching at the *secondary school* level but *not* at the elementary level	4	8	6
Others who are *not* certified	17	30	24

Note. Data refer to percentage of elementary school teachers with the specific teacher certifications. Totals equal more than 100% because respondents could check more than one response.

Table 38 and Figure 24 compare 1997 and 2008 data on the certifications of foreign language teachers at the elementary school level. Public and private elementary school teacher certification data are also compared. Results showed an increase in the percentage of elementary schools that had at least one teacher certified in foreign language teaching at the elementary level or for Grades K–12. This increase coincided with a decrease in the percentage of elementary schools with language teachers certified in foreign language teaching at the secondary level. At the same time, the percentage

Table 37. Certification of Elementary School Language Teachers (by Metro Status) (2008)

	Urban (%)	Suburban (%)	Rural (%)
Uncertified			
Public	13	12	37
Private	32	30	29
Certified in elementary education			
Public	15	17	32
Private	12	19	19

Table 38. Elementary Schools With at Least One Teacher With a Specific Certification (1997, 2008)

	Public		Private		Total	
TYPE OF CERTIFICATION	1997 (%)	2008 (%)	1997 (%)	2008 (%)	1997 (%)	2008 (%)
Elementary school teaching, but *not* specifically for foreign language	26	25	23	24	26	24
Foreign language teaching at the elementary school level	20	26	16	21	19	24
Foreign language teaching at the elementary school level *and* for elementary school teaching	20	27	12	12	15	19
Foreign language teaching at the K–12 level	22	40	12	30	19	34
Foreign language teaching at the *secondary school* level but *not* at the elementary level	13	7	16	8	15	8
Others who are *not* certified	8	19	19	40	12	31
High school/college students (1997 only)	6	–	3	–	5	–

Note. Data refer to percentage of elementary schools with one or more teachers with the specific teacher qualifications. Totals equal more than 100% because respondents could check more than one response. Dash (–) = data not collected in 2008.

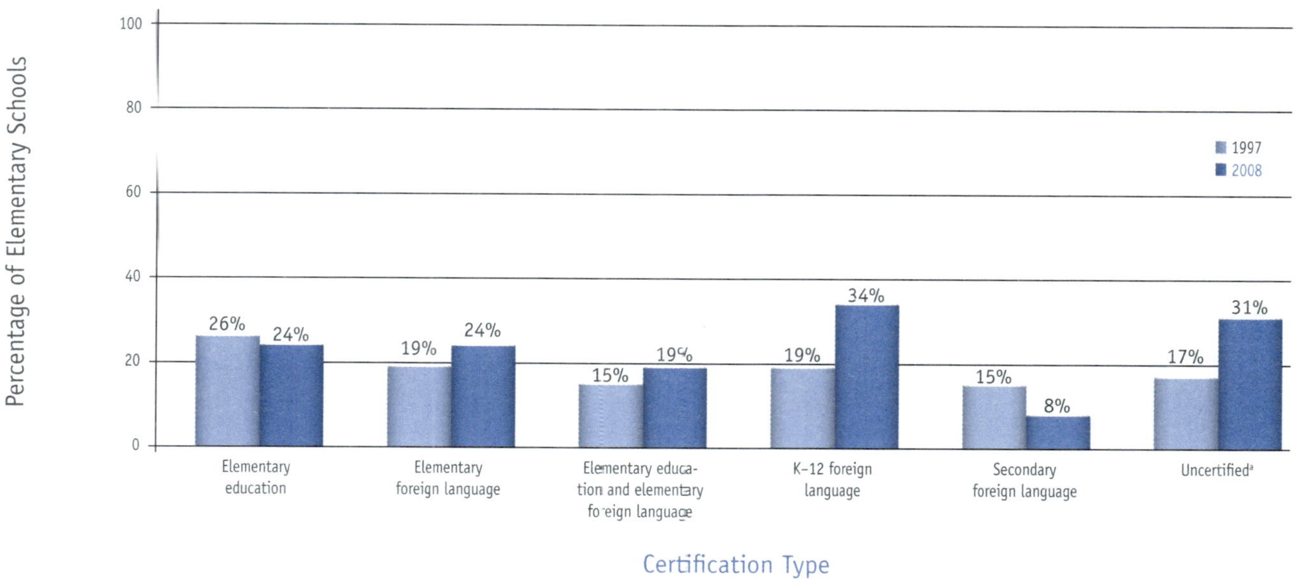

Figure 24. Elementary Schools With at Least One Teacher With a Specific Certification (1997, 2008).
[a]Uncertified teachers in 1997 included high school/college students.

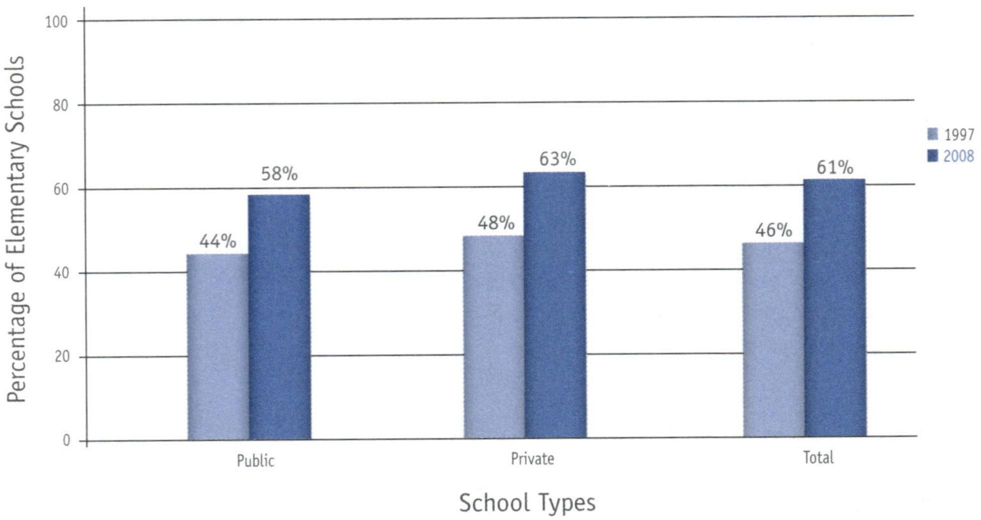

Figure 25. Elementary Schools With Foreign Language Programs That Have at Least One Native-Speaker Foreign Language Teacher (by School Type) (1997, 2008).

of schools using uncertified teachers increased from 17% to 31%. In public schools, the increase was small, from 14% to 19%. In private schools, the percentage nearly doubled, from 21% to 40%.

In 2008, a greater percentage of elementary schools reported that one or more of their foreign language teachers were native speakers of the language being taught (61%) than in 1997 (46%). This was true of both public and private schools (Figure 25).

Secondary Schools

In 2008, 94% of secondary foreign language teachers were certified and 6% were not (public 98% certified, 2% not; private 81% certified, 19% not). The majority were certified for foreign language teaching at the secondary level; 35% were certified for foreign language teaching at the K–12 level (Table 39). School size was directly related to teacher certification (86% of teachers at small schools were certified, 94% at medium schools, 97% at large schools, 99% at very large schools), but there was no variation across other variables. Table 40 and Figure

Table 39. Certifications of Secondary School Foreign Language Teachers (2008)

	Public (%)	Private (%)	Total (%)
Foreign language teaching at the secondary school level	79	47	72
Foreign language teaching at the K–12 level	35	32	35
More than one foreign language	10	7	9
Secondary school teaching, but *not* specifically for foreign language	6	9	6
Recognized as National Board Certified	6	3	5
A different foreign language from the one they teach	3	1	3
Foreign language teaching at the elementary school level but *not* at the secondary level	1	3	1
Others who are *not* certified	2	19	6

Note. Data refer to percentage of secondary school foreign language teachers with specific teacher certification. Totals equal more than 100% because respondents could check more than one response.

26 compare 1997 and 2008 data on the certification of foreign language teachers in secondary schools. In 2008, more schools had teachers with K-12 foreign language certification and fewer schools had teachers certified in more than one foreign language. Typically, public secondary schools were more likely than private secondary schools to report having at least one teacher certified in foreign language teaching.

A greater percentage of secondary schools in 2008 (44%) than in 1997 (33%) reported that one or more of their foreign language teachers were native speakers of the language being taught (Figure 27.) However, secondary schools were less likely than elementary schools to have foreign language teachers who were native speakers: 44% of secondary schools reported at least one native-speaker language teacher compared to 61% of elementary schools.

Table 40. Secondary Schools With at Least One Foreign Language Teacher With a Specific Certification (1997, 2008)

	Public		Private		Total	
TYPE OF CERTIFICATION	1997 (%)	2008 (%)	1997 (%)	2008 (%)	1997 (%)	2008 (%)
Secondary school teaching, but *not* specifically for foreign language	7	9	16	20	9	11
Foreign language teaching at the secondary school level	84	82	77	58	82	77
Foreign language teaching at the K-12 level	26	42	21	36	25	40
Foreign language teaching at the elementary school level but *not* at the secondary level	2	1	8	8	3	3
A different foreign language from the one they teach	9	7	8	3	9	6
More than one foreign language	35	22	34	14	34	20
Recognized as National Board Certified	–	7	–	4	–	7
Others who are *not* certified	8	6	33	30	11	12

Note. Data refer to percentage of secondary schools with one or more teachers with the specific teacher certifications. Totals equal more than 100% because respondents could check more than one response. Data (–) = data not collected in 1997.

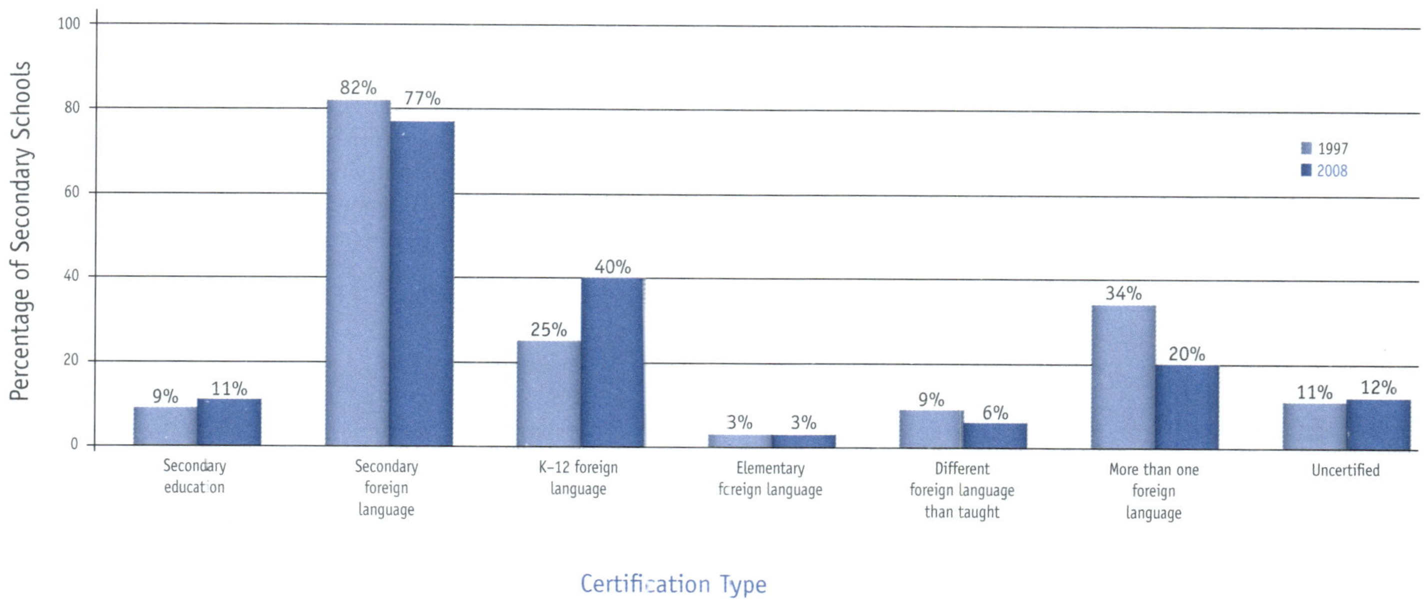

Figure 26. Secondary Schools With at Least One Foreign Language Teacher With a Specific Qualification (1997, 2008).

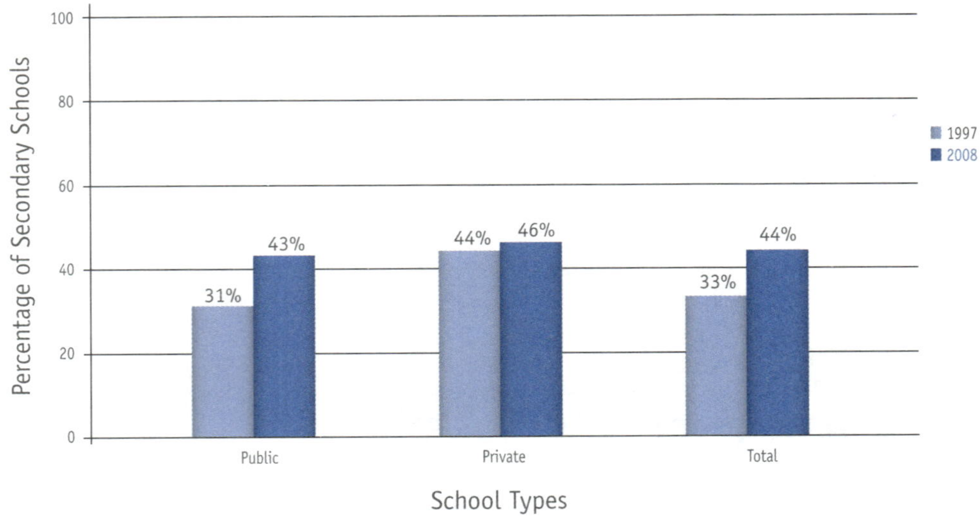

Figure 27. Secondary Schools With Foreign Language Programs That Have at Least One Native-Speaker Foreign Language Teacher (by School Type) (1997, 2008).

Professional Development and Inservice Training

As in the two previous surveys, respondents were asked whether any of the language teachers at their school had participated in professional development or inservice teacher training during the previous 12 months. However, unlike the 1987 and 1997 surveys, the 2008 survey asked specifically about professional development in the language teachers' subject area.

Elementary Schools

In 2008, 63% of elementary schools with foreign language programs reported that their language teachers had participated in professional development or inservice training in their subject area during the previous 12 months (Figure 28.) As during previous survey periods, the percentage of public elementary school teachers participating in professional development in 2008 was higher than the percentage of private elementary school teachers. The level of participation in professional development did not vary according to geographic region but it did vary by all other variables.

Rural schools reported much lower participation in professional development than suburban and urban schools, and smaller schools reported lower participation than larger schools (Table 41). Levels of participation were also correlated to levels of minority enrollment and socioeconomic status: In general, as the number of minority students or students from low socioeconomic backgrounds increased, teachers' levels of participation in professional development also increased.

Secondary Schools

At the secondary level, 73% of schools with foreign language programs (public and private combined) reported that their language teachers had attended professional development in their subject area within the preceding 12 months. This did not represent a statistically significant difference from 1997. However, while the level of public school professional development remained stable from 1997 to 2008, the level at private schools decreased (Figure 29).

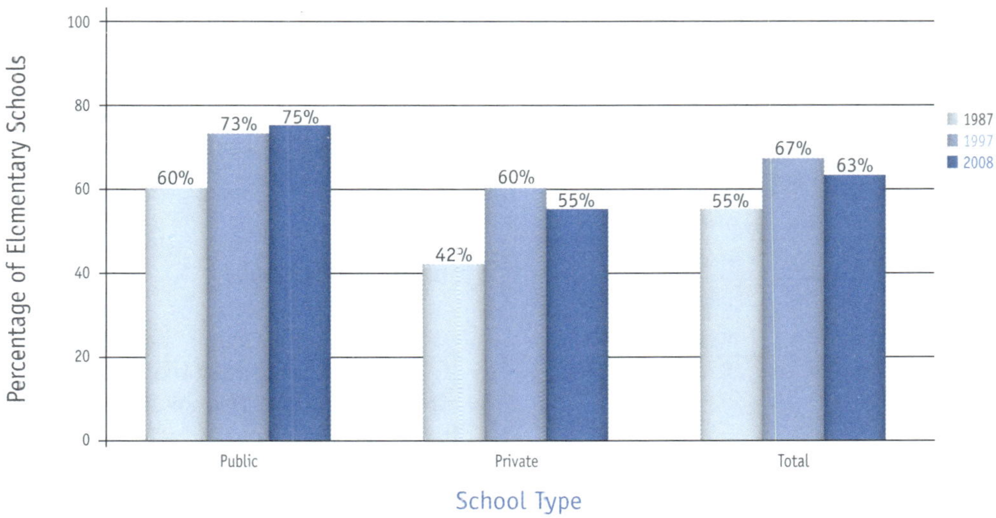

Figure 28. Elementary Schools With Foreign Language Teachers Participating in Professional Development/Inservice Training (by School Type) (1987, 1997, 2008).

Note. Differences between 1997 and 2008 were not statistically significant.

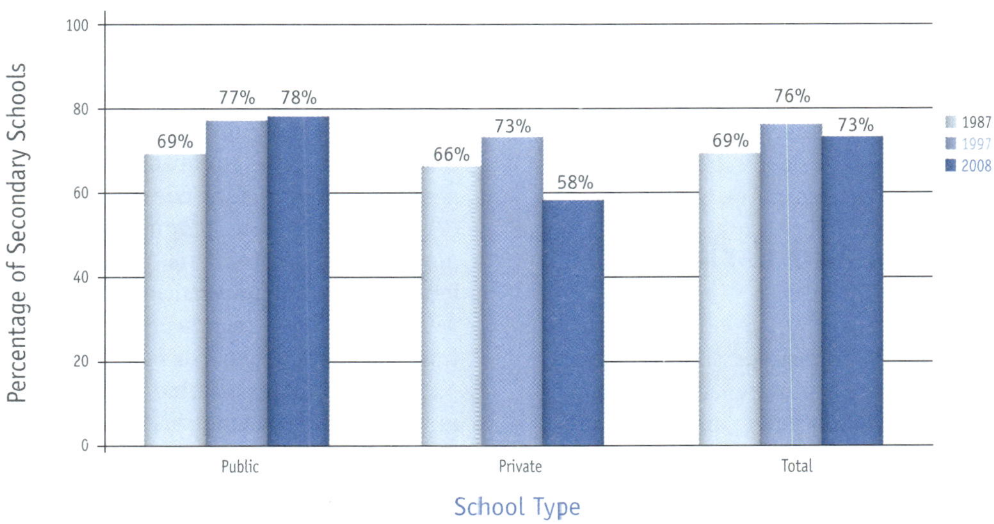

Figure 29. Secondary Schools With Foreign Language Teachers Participating in Professional Development/Inservice Training (by School Type) (1987, 1997, 2008).

Note. Differences between 1997 and 2008 were not statistically significant.

Table 41. Elementary School Foreign Language Teachers' Participation in Professional Development (by SES, Minority Enrollment, and School Size) (2008)

SES		Minority enrollment		School size	
Levels	(%)	Levels	(%)	Levels	(%)
Very low	89	Low	60	Small	55
Low	75	Medium	55	Medium	77
Medium	55	High	64	Large	88
High	70	Very high	78	Very large	80

Note. Data for SES are provided for public schools only.

In 1997, more high schools (84%) than middle schools (68%) reported teacher participation in professional development; in 2008, those percentages were nearly reversed (83% for middle school vs. 70% for high school). Participation in professional development was higher in urban and suburban schools (80% and 82%) than in rural schools (63%), and it was higher in medium, large, and very large schools (ranging from 81% to 93%) than in small schools (54%). Rates of participation also increased with levels of minority enrollment (69% low, 70% medium, 75% high, 83% very high). There was some variation across geographic conference regions: Northeast 81%, Southwest 75%, Central States 72%, Southern 67%, and Pacific Northwest 65%.

Teacher Shortages and Hiring Practices

The two questions related to teacher shortages were new in the 2008 survey. They were added because many states and school districts had reported problems finding and hiring qualified foreign language teachers (Bousquet, 1999; Murphy, DeArmond, & Guin, 2003). First, elementary and secondary schools that offered foreign language instruction were asked whether they had been affected by a shortage of qualified foreign language teachers and, if yes, to explain how they had been affected. Second, elementary schools—which have reported particular difficulty finding qualified language teachers (Rhodes & Branaman, 1999)—were asked whether any of the school's foreign language teachers had been hired through alternative means (e.g., through agencies that provide teachers from other countries, commercial language schools, foreign governments). If the answer was yes, schools were asked to elaborate.

Elementary Schools

Of all elementary schools that offered foreign languages in 2008, 25% responded that they had been affected by a teacher shortage (Figure 30). There was no difference between public and private schools; however, more rural schools (34%) reported that they were affected by a shortage than did urban (23%) or suburban schools (22%). While there was no variation by school size or minority enrollment, there was a correlation with socioeconomic status. Forty percent of very low SES schools but only 17% of high SES schools were affected by a teacher shortage. Geographic region was also a factor, with schools in the Pacific Northwest and Central States regions being most affected by teacher shortages (31% for each) and schools in the Southern region the least (16%).

One way that elementary schools were coping with teacher shortages was by finding and hiring teachers through nontraditional means. Schools listed four alternative means of recruiting teachers: (1) hiring teachers from other countries by working with domestic agencies or with ministries of foreign governments, (2) contracting with proprietary language schools to provide language teachers, (3) hiring instructors from local colleges and universities, and (4) sharing teachers with other schools (e.g., a private school hiring teachers from the public schools in a shared arrangement). Of all elementary schools offering language instruction, 10% reported hiring a language teacher using alternative means. Public schools, especially urban public schools, were more likely than private schools to hire teachers through alternative means.

Thirty-nine elementary schools (18 private, 21 public) provided details about how they hired teachers through alternative means. Eleven of the public elementary schools reported recruiting teachers from other countries, either through arrangements with foreign governments or through agencies that provide teachers from overseas, while only two of the private schools reported having done so. The following sources of teachers from other countries were mentioned by respondents:

- Governments of China, France, Greece, Italy, Portugal, and Spain
- Agencies that provide teachers from other countries
- VIF (Visiting International Faculty) Program, an exchange program for teachers from abroad who want to teach in the United States
- Canadian teacher training programs
- Foreign educational organizations

Five private school respondents, but only one public school respondent, reported hiring language teachers from proprietary language schools. Specific proprietary schools mentioned were Language Adventure Programs, Futura Language Professionals, and International Academy.

Three schools (two private, one public) reported finding teachers through local colleges or universities. One school had contracted with a local community college to provide one or more language teachers. Another reported hiring a Chinese instructor from a nearby state university, and another had hired a local college student to teach Italian. Three private schools in Michigan reported participating in a shared-time program with public schools, in which teachers from the local public school district provided instruction for the private school students in various electives, including foreign languages.

The remaining comments about alternative means of hiring included general observations as well as explanations of who, other than foreign language teachers, taught foreign languages at the respondents' schools (e.g., independent teacher, volunteer, regular classroom teacher, principal, paraprofessional) and how those teachers were paid (e.g., grants, stipends from the PTA).

Comments about teacher shortages were received from 99 elementary school respondents (44 public, 55 private), the vast majority (87%) from schools that had been affected by a shortage of qualified language teachers. These are some of the comments from public school respondents whose schools had been affected:

> "Absolutely. We would not be subcontracting out to private language schools for our teachers if there were qualified teachers available."

> "It is difficult to find qualified teachers that are certified to teach in Spanish."

> "More time exposure would lead to more fluency... impossible with one teacher and 600 students."

> "There are simply few people who speak the language [Hupa] here. Only a dozen or so fluent elders are still with us and fewer still are those who have been learning the languages enough to teach them; although those that have are a very dedicated bunch and more are coming along all the time thanks to our program."

> "We are often hiring late into the summer due to lack of available and qualified candidates.

"We would not be subcontracting out to private language schools for our teachers if there were qualified teachers available."

This can result in hiring candidates who are not well prepared, but who are available."

The following comments came from private school respondents whose schools had been affected by a shortage of qualified language teachers:

> "It is difficult to find teachers who simply specialize in that area. In addition, due to the nature of a private school, faculty often wears many hats. So while we do have faculty that are very qualified to teach foreign language it is not always as easy nor always cost effective to fill for an instructor who only teaches a foreign language."

> "It is hard to find Hebrew teachers with certification."

> "Most teachers prefer teaching in a public school setting because of salary and instructional benefits."

Even some of the respondents who claimed not to have been affected by the teacher shortage qualified their responses with comments such as these:

> "[No], but it is always very hard to replace a good foreign language teacher when they go, especially Korean."

> "No, but at times it has been difficult to find the right teacher."

And then there are those few schools that are just plain lucky:

> "Not at all . . . the two of us [language teachers] are fantastic!"

Secondary Schools

At the secondary school level, 30% of schools offering foreign languages reported being affected by a shortage of qualified language teachers (Figure 30). Middle schools (32%) were slightly more affected than high schools (28%); private high schools (35%), particularly in rural areas, were more affected than public high schools (25%). No variation by region, school size, or minority enrollment was observed, but, as was true of public elementary schools, there was a direct correlation between socioeconomic status and teacher shortages: Lower SES schools faced more teacher shortages than higher SES schools. In addition, there was variation across geographic regions, with schools in the Northeast reporting the largest effect (42%), followed by the Pacific Northwest (30%), Southern (28%), Central States (26%), and Southwest regions (24%).

Written comments were received from 127 secondary school respondents (72 public, 55 private), 86% of whom answered that their school had been affected by a shortage of qualified teachers. The following are examples of comments received from affected public school respondents:

> "Hard to find native Spanish speakers to come to Alaska."

> "At times less competent teachers had to be hired due to shortage of candidates."

> "I called 12 different colleges seeking a foreign language teacher. We now have a teacher who is on a certified waiver."

> "Japanese teachers are difficult to find."

> "Classes in Japanese and Latin will be eliminated if the part-time faculty teachers cannot be found."

Even public school respondents whose schools had not been affected by a shortage of teachers reported potential problems:

> "We are concerned about filling openings when retirements occur."

> "Ours is a [small] school district and only one Spanish teacher is needed. However, other surrounding, much larger districts are in dire

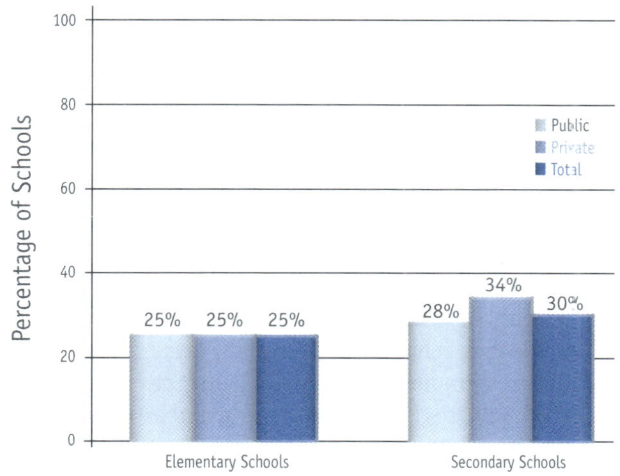

Figure 30. Elementary and Secondary Schools That Currently Teach Foreign Languages That Are Affected by a Shortage of Qualified Foreign Language Teachers (2008).

need of Spanish teachers and are not filling those positions."

Among private school respondents who reported that their schools had been affected by a shortage of qualified teachers, several mentioned a wide range of related issues in their comments, including non-ideal teaching situations, amount of work, part-time versus full-time employment, and inadequate compensation.

> "Hard to find Latin and German teachers, especially those who want to work part time."

> "It is practically impossible to locate and interview 'new' teachers. We have two openings at present and cannot find anyone to fill these vacancies."

> "Since it is difficult to find qualified teachers for foreign language, we have to resort to more video curriculum or not offer foreign language."

> "We recruit native speakers and it is often difficult to find native speakers who are certified in their country of origin. We travel abroad to find native speakers as well as advertise locally, but it can be difficult to attract foreign candidates to [our Midwestern city]."

> "There are horror stories where they hire English teachers to try to teach Spanish. Lack of quality applicants is a great concern."

These comments are from private secondary school respondents who reported that their schools had not been affected by a shortage of language teachers:

> "Our Chinese teachers are not certified but are very experienced in teaching Chinese. The primary Chinese teacher has received many awards from the [professional association] including 'best teacher' and 'best senior teacher.' We are satisfied about most of our students' progress."

> "The problem at our school has more to do with time available in the school program for foreign language instruction."

Discussion

Survey results revealed differences between public and private schools in the number of foreign language teachers employed. These differences are most likely a reflection of the types of programs offered. For example, immersion programs, which require a large number of language teachers, were offered by more public schools than private schools, hence the greater percentage of public elementary schools with more than six foreign language teachers. Exploratory programs, which may need only one teacher, were also offered by more public than private schools, hence the greater percentage of public schools with only one language teacher. Language focus programs, which typically require more than one language teacher per school but not nearly as many teachers as immersion programs, were found more often in private schools than public schools, hence the higher percentage of private schools having between three and five language teachers. Private schools also tended to have a higher percentage of students enrolled in language classes than public schools, and they tended to have smaller class sizes, both of which require a larger number of teachers. For example, at the secondary level, the ratio of language students to language teachers was 39 to 1 for private schools compared to 79 to 1 for public schools.

The percentage of elementary schools offering foreign languages without the benefit of a foreign language teacher decreased from 1997 to 2008, suggesting that the quality of instruction and the professionalization of foreign language teaching may have improved. On the other hand, the highest percentage of both elementary and secondary schools offering languages reported having only one foreign language teacher, thus confirming the professional isolation of these teachers (Hammadou & Bernhardt, 1987; Sadow, 1996). They have limited opportunities to engage in professional exchange with their peers, which in some instances may lead to their leaving the profession and contributing to a shortage of qualified teachers (Bousquet, 1999). Access to professional development is therefore particularly important for language teachers to increase both their personal job satisfaction and their involvement in the profession, leading to enhanced instruction and increased teacher retention.

Although most schools (63% elementary, 73% secondary) reported that their teachers had engaged in subject-specific professional development within the previous year, the level of participation at both the elementary and secondary levels remained unchanged between 1997 and 2008. A cause for concern is the disparity in professional development between rural schools and urban and suburban schools, with teachers in rural schools—who were more likely than their urban or suburban counterparts to be the only language teacher in their school—having a much lower rate of participation. A similar disparity existed between small and larger schools. It is interesting to note that participation in professional development was higher among teachers in schools with large populations of minority students or students from low socioeconomic backgrounds.

Survey results show that of all elementary school language teachers in the United States, more than one quarter were not certified at all. In fact, the percentage of schools that reported having uncertified language teachers increased from 17% in 1997 to 31% in 2008. At the same time, the percentage of schools that reported having at least one teacher with certification in foreign language teaching at the elementary or K–12 level increased. In 1997, 19% reported having at least one teacher certified for K–12 and 19% reported having at least one teacher certified for elementary school foreign language teaching; in 2008 the percentages were 34% and 24%, respectively.

In comparison, the overwhelming majority of secondary schools reported that their language teachers were certified, with 77% certified for foreign language teaching at the secondary level and 40% certified for foreign language teaching at the K–12 level. (Teachers could list more than one certification.) The percentage of schools reporting that instruction was provided by noncertified teachers remained the same (about 10%) between 1997 and 2008.

The language teacher shortages reported here confirm shortages reported in a survey of northeastern schools for the 2003–2004 school year (Rosenbusch & Jensen, 2005). The respondents' comments provide

A cause for concern is the disparity in professional development between rural schools and urban and suburban schools, with teachers in rural schools having a much lower rate of participation.

useful insight into the challenges of finding qualified language teachers. Schools' main concerns focused on a shortage of (1) qualified language teachers in general; (2) teachers within a particular school (too many students per teacher); (3) teachers of specific languages, especially less commonly taught languages; and (4) qualified substitute teachers. Other challenges mentioned included rapid teacher turnover, difficulty attracting language teachers to specific geographical areas (Alaska and Indiana were both mentioned), and certification issues, including the issue of hiring overseas-trained, native-speaker teachers without U.S. certification.

Information from elementary schools about whether they used alternative means to hire foreign language teachers provided more insight into the extent to which schools were affected by a teacher shortage and how they dealt with it. Ten percent of elementary schools that taught languages reported having hired teachers through alternative means; public schools more often relied on recruiting foreign teachers whereas private schools were more likely to use proprietary language schools. Data from both questions along with the respondents' comments represented tangible and quantifiable evidence to support the long-standing argument that university programs need to augment and improve the preparation and training of K–12 language teachers (Schrier, 2001). Improving the language teaching situation (and thus encouraging more prospective teachers into the profession), in elementary schools in particular, requires a systematic initiative aimed at increasing the number of highly qualified teachers in a wide range of languages.

At the same time, it is necessary to improve the status, training, and working conditions of all language teachers. The rationale for the professionalization of foreign language teaching is that it will lead to more committed and motivated teachers, which will improve teachers' performance, and thus, ultimately, student learning (see National Center for Education Statistics, 1997; Talbert & McLaughlin, 1993).

CHAPTER 7: EDUCATIONAL REFORM

This chapter provides results on the implementation of national and state foreign language standards and the effects of the No Child Left Behind (NCLB) education legislation on language instruction. These results provide key details on how educational reform has affected foreign language teaching in the schools. Results for each section are presented first for elementary schools, then for secondary schools.

Standards for Foreign Language Learning

Elementary Schools

In 2008, 59% of elementary schools that taught foreign languages reported that their foreign language teachers routinely integrated the national foreign language standards and/or state standards into their instruction (Figure 31). This was a large increase from 1997, when 19% of schools reported having changed their foreign language curriculum as a result of their awareness of the standards.[21] Public schools were much more likely to follow national or state standards than private schools, but both posted notable increases from 1997. Standards integration varied little by metro status, minority enrollment, or socioeconomic status, but school size was a factor. Very large schools reported more standards integration than large, medium, or small schools (91%, 66%, 76%, and 52%, respectively). As was true in 1997, schools in the Northeast Conference region reported the highest use of standards: 71% compared to just over 50% in each of the other regions.

In 1997, survey respondents who offered comments on the standards wrote about the process of implementing them, whereas in 2008, the majority of the 50 respondents (20 public, 30 private) simply named the standards they were using. This was particularly the case for public school respondents, but it was also true of nearly half of the private school respondents. This type of response may be an indication that a detailed discussion of standards implementation was not viewed as critical in 2008, when national standards had been in place for many years. As one private school respondent commented: "We integrate [the standards] not because we have to, but because they make sense for teaching language."

Comments from public school respondents who did not integrate national or state standards into their instruction (3 out of 20) provided explanations for their lack of standards use, such as their language program being new but that they were planning to use the standards in the future, or not having enough time to integrate all the standards. Several private schools that did not follow state or national standards provided similar explanations, while others said that they used other standards (e.g., IB Primary Years, French government standards). Only two private schools reported that they were not aware of the national foreign language standards.

Secondary Schools

Of all secondary schools with language programs, 83% reported that their foreign language teachers integrated the foreign language standards into their instruction, an increase from 1997, when 30% of schools reported having changed their curriculum in response to the creation of the national standards (Figure 32). While a higher percentage of public schools

[21] Because of a change in wording of the standards question in 2008, the 1997 data were recalculated for comparability purposes to reflect percentage of schools that offered foreign languages, were aware of the standards, and had changed their curriculum because of awareness of the standards.

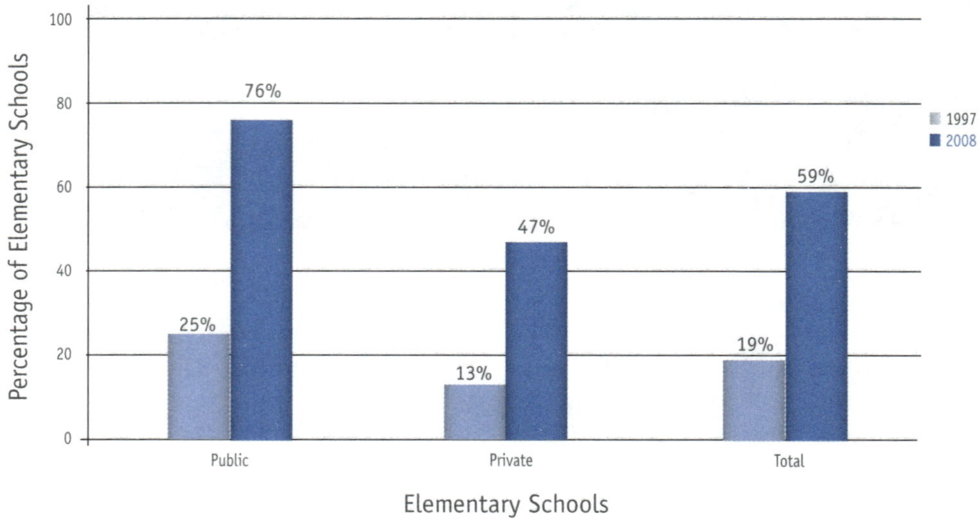

Figure 31. Elementary Schools That Integrate the National Standards or State Standards Into Foreign Language Instruction (by School Type) (1997, 2008).
Note. No statistical tests were conducted on these data.

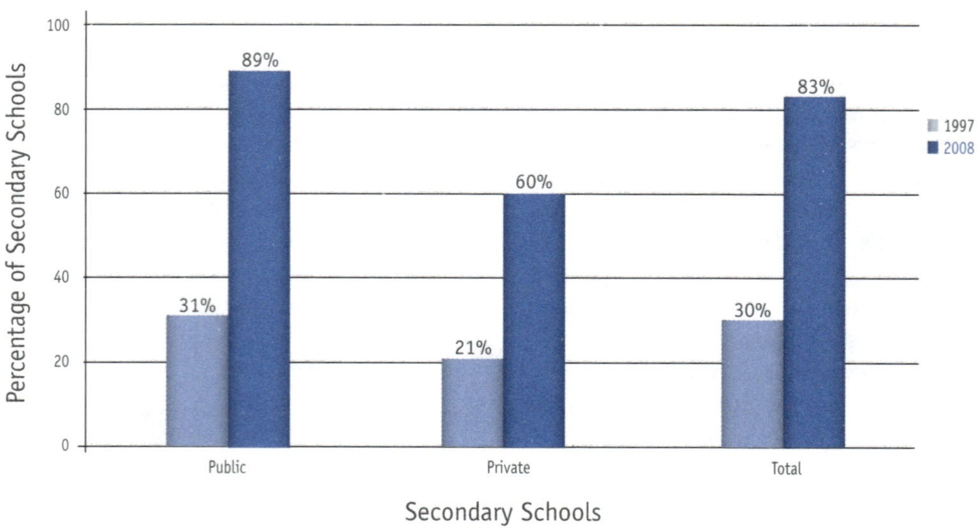

Figure 32. Secondary Schools That Integrate the National Standards/State Standards Into Instruction (by School Type) (1997, 2008).
Note. No statistical tests were conducted on these data.

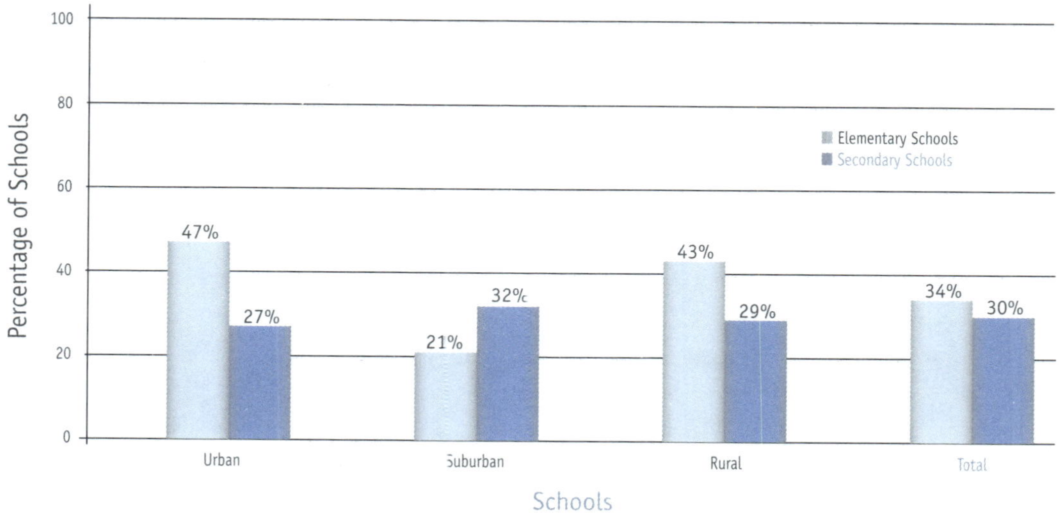

Figure 33. Public Elementary and Secondary Schools With Foreign Language Programs That Were Affected by NCLB (by Metro Status) (2008).

than private schools reported the use of national or state standards in 2008, the increase at both types of schools is noteworthy. There was relatively little variation in standards use among urban, suburban, and rural secondary schools, but there was variation among schools of different sizes. Small schools were less likely to integrate the standards than medium, large, or very large schools (65% compared to 92%, 92%, and 99%, respectively). Schools in the Northeast Conference region (90%) were most likely to integrate standards in their foreign language instruction, followed by the Southern, Southwest, and Central States regions (all 82%) and the Pacific Northwest region (76%). Schools with a high minority enrollment were more likely to integrate standards than schools with lower minority enrollment (91% compared to a range of 80% to 83%). Low SES schools were less likely to integrate standards than higher SES schools.

The relatively few comments offered by public secondary schools mostly identified the specific standards that were used. Some comments from private secondary schools were very specific, for example, "Connections [one of the national standards—connecting with other disciplines] is the focus of our curriculum. Art, Literature, and History are taught in the target language, even in level 1." Other private school respondents admitted to complete unawareness of the national standards, for example, "I have no idea what these are."

No Child Left Behind

Following the recommendation of professionals in the field, a new question was added to the 2008 survey asking respondents if NCLB, signed into law in 2002, had affected foreign language instruction at their schools. Because private schools are not bound by the mandates of this federal education legislation, this discussion will focus mainly on results from public schools.

Elementary Schools

Of all public elementary schools that offered foreign languages, 34% reported that their foreign language instruction had been affected by NCLB (Figure 33). Urban and rural schools were more likely to be affected than suburban schools, and lower SES schools were more affected than higher SES schools (Figure 34). In addition, schools with a very high minority enrollment

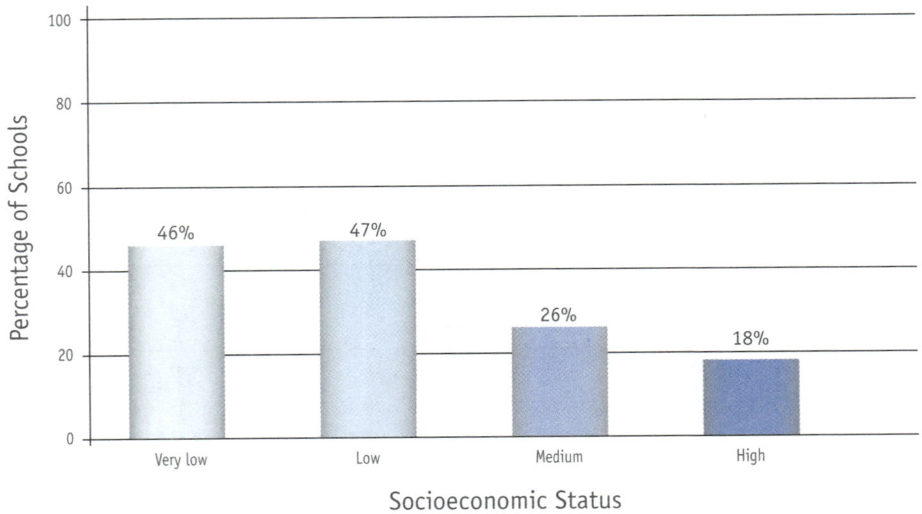

Figure 34. Public Elementary Schools With Foreign Language Programs That Were Affected by NCLB (by Socioeconomic Status) (2008).

Note. No statistical tests were conducted on these data. Very low SES school = ≥ 70% of students eligible for free or reduced-price lunch; low SES = 40%–69% eligible; medium SES = 20%–39% eligible; high SES = < 20% eligible.

(more than 50%) were more likely to report being affected by NCLB than schools with a lower minority enrollment (Table 42). A small percentage (2%) of private elementary schools reported that they, too, had been affected by NCLB.

We received written comments from 71 elementary schools (55 public, 16 private) in response to the question, "Has foreign language instruction in your school been affected by No Child Left Behind legislation?" Of the 55 public elementary schools that provided comments, 87% reported that foreign language instruction at their school had been impacted by NCLB. Of those, 85% explicitly noted that the impacts were negative:

> "More time is spent on English and math than foreign language because of NCLB."

> "Funds and time have been directed to reading and math. In some cases, we pull students from foreign language and other non tested content classes in order to provide more extensive reading and math support."

Table 42. Public Elementary Schools With Foreign Language Programs That Were Affected by NCLB (by Minority Enrollment) (2008)

	Minority enrollment				
	Low	Medium	High	Very high	All schools
Schools affected	28%	25%	36%	42%	34%

Note. Low = < 10% minority enrollment; medium = 10%–29% minority enrollment; high = 30%–49% minority enrollment; very high = ≥ 50% minority enrollment.

> "Negative impact. So much focus on math and reading that there's not enough time for other important subjects."

The remaining 15% who were affected by NCLB, but not explicitly negatively, noted issues such as certification requirements and changes in classroom activities or curriculum:

> "Modified activities so all students can achieve success in class."

> "We have had to update our curriculum so that it aligns more with classroom bench marks. Also, we have been asked to incorporate more writing into our curriculum. Our state has legislated that all students be proficient in a second world language by the year 2016. Therefore, all students must have two credits in world language to be awarded their high school diploma. Within the next 2 years, our district will be revising our curriculum in the K–12 grades to meet this requirement using the state guidelines."

One school reported how they were coping with the constraints imposed by NCLB:

> "When our district is faced with budget cuts (now every year), we are put on the chopping block since Math, Language Arts, and now Science are more important, and FLES is a luxury. Fortunately, with a supportive School Board and a focus on content-related instruction (teaching key objectives from the SCOS for Math, Language Arts, and Science through French) we have been able to maintain our excellent program. Rather than lament and complain about the NCLB legislation, we've been proactive and made it work for us. Although I will say the constant advocacy our program demands can be exhausting and does take away valuable time and energy from our students."

Secondary Schools

Of all public secondary schools with foreign language programs, 30% reported that their programs had been affected by NCLB (Figure 33). There was little variation across metro status or SES, and there were no major differences between middle schools and high schools. However, schools with a higher minority enrollment were more likely to be affected by NCLB than those with a low minority enrollment (Table 43).

One hundred secondary school respondents (75 public, 25 private) provided written comments. Again, because private schools are not bound by NCLB, the focus here is on comments from public schools. Of the public secondary school respondents who provided comments, 93% reported that foreign language instruction in their school had been affected by NCLB. Of these, 91% cited negative effects:

> "Attention focused on core subjects due to NCLB legislation has caused depleted resources and opportunities in foreign language."

> "Fewer children are taking foreign language because they have to focus on other areas."

> "I have smaller classes because if a student does not perform well on the assessments they must lose an elective and take extra math and reading courses. And I do not get to attend as

Table 43. Public Secondary Schools With Foreign Language Programs That Were Affected by NCLB (by Minority Enrollment) (2008)

	Minority enrollment				
	Low	Medium	High	Very high	All schools
Schools affected	20%	40%	26%	34%	30%

Note. Low = < 10% minority enrollment; medium = 10%–29% minority enrollment; high = 30%–49% minority enrollment; very high = ≥ 50% minority enrollment.

many professional conferences, because reading and math must come first. We're also encouraged to give multiple choice tests to increase skills in taking those kinds of tests, but that is not the ideal way to assess foreign language."

"We used to be a leader in foreign language in our school system. We offered French, Spanish, Latin, German, Russian, and Japanese. Because of budget cuts due to things like NCLB and our state ISTEP test/remediation, etc., we have been reduced to just French and Spanish."

"Our Japanese language teacher did not make 'Highly Qualified Status' and we had to lose the program."

"Many of our higher achieving students, those who traditionally are enrolled in foreign language at the middle school level, have left the school through NCLB Choice [where students select to attend a higher performing school because home school was identified as needing improvement]."

A few public secondary schools (9%) commented on positive impacts of NCLB, such as support for students, curriculum, and classroom activities:

"We offer after-school assistance."

"Rewrote the curriculum based on standards, both state and national."

"Greater attention to data analysis, use of proven teaching methods, use of newer, more effective methods for learning such as TPRS [Teaching Proficiency through Reading and Storytelling]."

The comment below is from one of the few schools that reported no effects from NCLB:

"Not really [affected], because our school is a Magnet Program School and we already had in place and functioning many of the components that were incorporated into the No Child Left Behind legislation."

Discussion

The national foreign language standards are designed to help teachers help their students develop high levels of proficiency in the languages they study. The standards include five goals: communication in languages other than English, knowledge and understanding of other cultures, connection with other disciplines, comparisons allowing insight into the nature of language and culture, and participation in multilingual communities at home and around the world (National Standards in Foreign Language Education Project, 2006). These standards are intended to serve as a gauge for excellence, as states and local districts implement curriculum in the schools. One of the most promising findings of this survey is the large increase in the percentage of schools that have incorporated the national or state foreign language standards into their instruction. At both the

"Attention focused on core subjects due to NCLB legislation has caused depleted resources and opportunities in foreign language."

elementary and secondary levels, the percentage of schools using student standards almost tripled from 1997 to 2008. This is an indication that schools across the country have come to more of a consensus on the essential skills and knowledge that should be acquired in language classes and have set high goals to match the standards.

In contrast to this good news, survey results reveal that NCLB has had a negative effect on foreign language instruction in many schools. Approximately one third of public elementary and secondary schools teaching foreign languages reported negative effects. At the elementary level, low SES schools were more affected than higher SES schools. Comments from respondents suggested that the intense focus on the NCLB tested subjects—mathematics and reading—had depleted resources and time that had formerly been spent on foreign languages. Additionally, many experienced teachers, especially those who taught uncommonly taught languages, were negatively affected by the highly qualified requirements specified in NCLB (Assembly Committee on Education, 2006; Atkins, Supahan, & Lewis, 2008).

CAL survey results confirm the findings of other studies. Rosenbusch and Jensen (2005, p. 33) found that since the enactment of NCLB in 2002, the lack of qualified teachers (as defined by NCLB) and a focus on the testing of mathematics and reading skills have been important factors in the elimination of foreign language teaching positions and the cutting of language programs. These findings were echoed by the Center on Education Policy (Marzo, 2008), which found that NCLB has marginalized many subjects, including foreign languages, because they are not included in its accountability measures. The Center reports that more than half of all school districts increased reading and math instruction between 2001 and 2007 while significantly reducing instruction in other subjects (p. 1). The results of CAL's survey are in keeping with the findings of these earlier studies.

PART 4
Conclusion

CHAPTER 8: CONCLUSIONS AND RECOMMENDATIONS

The profile of foreign language instruction in the United States revealed by CAL's 2008 survey shows that foreign language instruction has remained relatively stable at the high school level over the past decade but that it has decreased substantially in elementary and middle schools nationwide. Moreover, only a small percentage of the elementary and middle schools not teaching languages in 2008 planned to implement a language program within the next 2 years.

These results are disappointing. The United States is at a point in history when, as Gene R. Carter (2008), Executive Director of ASCD (formerly the Association for Supervision and Curriculum Development), states, "At stake is whether an entire generation of learners will fail to make the grade in a global economy." At a time when countries around the world are implementing language programs for younger and younger children and are positioning their students to become multilingual world citizens of the 21st century (Education, Audiovisual and Culture Executive Agency, 2008), it seems incomprehensible that the United States is not making every effort to provide students with the early-start, long-sequence foreign language instruction that will prepare them to participate effectively in a globally competitive world.

Moreover, the educational reform efforts that resulted from the NCLB federal education law, which aimed to make U.S. students more globally competitive by focusing on mathematics and reading instruction, may well have had the opposite effect because of their unintended adverse effects on foreign language programs. Unless foreign language teaching with a strong alignment to national and state standards is recognized as an important priority for the nation, the decline in public schools offering languages is likely to continue, and most of our students will continue to be monolingual.

Survey data revealed a number of other disturbing trends:

- There were inequities in access to foreign language education. Languages were offered in smaller percentages of rural schools and low SES schools.
- The teaching of French, German, Japanese, and Russian decreased at both the elementary and secondary level.
- Nearly one third of public elementary and secondary schools with language programs reported that language teaching had been negatively affected by NCLB.
- The disparity between public and private elementary school language offerings increased exponentially, with private schools offering languages at much higher rates than public schools.
- The shortage of language teachers is so severe that some schools are having to find alternative sources of teachers, such as agencies that provide teachers from other countries, commercial language schools, and foreign governments that send teachers to the United States.

Several positive trends were also evident from the survey results:

- The teaching of Arabic and Chinese increased at both the elementary and secondary levels.
- Language teachers at both the elementary and secondary levels integrated national and state

language standards into their teaching more than they did a decade earlier and used the target language in the classroom more frequently.

- There are pockets of innovation—in particular immersion programs where elementary schools offer language instruction resulting in high levels of proficiency.
- More language classes used authentic literature from the target culture than before.
- The use of technology-based materials—Internet resources, computer-assisted instructional materials, instructional technology—has increased significantly.
- Both elementary and secondary schools continued to offer language classes for native speakers—mostly in Spanish, but in some other languages as well.

As was the case in 1997, there continues to be reason for serious concern about the limited number of long-sequence K–12 language programs designed to provide students with the linguistic and cultural skills needed to communicate effectively in the United States and abroad. Well-articulated elementary and secondary programs are still the exception rather than the rule, and intensive instruction that aims at a high level of proficiency is scarce. In addition, the gap has widened between the haves and the have-nots. Although instruction has improved for students whose schools offer foreign languages, a large number of elementary and middle school students in this country, especially those in rural or low SES schools, do not have the opportunity to study foreign language at all.

Finally, although the increase in the percentage of schools offering Spanish is a positive sign, it appears to be occurring at the expense of other languages. The proximity of the United States to Latin America and the growing number of Spanish-speaking U.S. citizens have made Spanish the language of choice in this country. While this is understandable, Spanish is not the only other language Americans need to know. For example, French and German are important for competition in the global economy. Knowledge of languages such as Chinese and Arabic is proving to be important to the United States for commerce and security reasons. Native American languages and other heritage languages are important to the preservation of the country's cultural vitality and heritage.

Recommendations

In the report of the 1987 survey results, the authors made five recommendations focused on developing more rigorous, long-sequence (K–12) foreign language programs whose goal would be for students to achieve communicative proficiency in the target language (Rhodes & Oxford, 1988). These recommendations were revisited 10 years later in light of the 1997 survey results, which showed some areas of progress along with areas of stagnation (Rhodes & Branaman, 1999). In reviewing these recommendations yet again in light of the 2008 survey results, we find that we have been losing ground over the past decade while showing progress in only a few areas. We therefore reiterate our original recommendations below, with some modifications and updated and expanded rationales. We also offer one new recommendation.

> *There continues to be reason for serious concern about the limited number of long-sequence K–12 language programs designed to provide students with the linguistic and cultural skills needed.*

Recommendation 1

Encourage the establishment of new foreign language programs, particularly those that start in the elementary school and aim at a high degree of proficiency.

Only 25% of elementary schools in the United States were offering foreign language instruction in 2008. This puts our country far behind much of the rest of the world in providing foreign language instruction for our children (Pufahl, Rhodes, & Christian, 2000). The educational community began to address this issue two decades ago, as reflected in the 1997 survey results: an increase of almost 10 percentage points from 1987 to 1997 in the percentage of elementary schools teaching foreign languages. This increase was spurred in large part by a grass-roots movement of community activists, parents, and local school officials (Heining-Boynton, 1990; Taboada, 2004; Viadero, 1991) assisted by such organizations as the National Network for Early Language Learning, the American Council on the Teaching of Foreign Languages, the Northeast Conference on the Teaching of Foreign Languages, and the Second/Foreign Language Acquisition by Children Conference. In addition, parents received advocacy help from such organizations as Advocates for Language Learning and the National Parent Teacher Association.

There is evidence that as recently as 2004, language programs for young students were still going strong (J. D. Edwards, personal communication, April 30, 2009; Rhodes & Gilzow, 2005). One of the major factors that seems to have led to a decrease in foreign language programs after 2004 is the enactment of the federal education law, NCLB, in 2002 (Rosenbusch & Jensen, 2005; see also chapter 7 in this volume). Its focus on math and reading has led some school districts to cut subjects like foreign languages, which are not tested under NCLB, in order to shift more resources into the subjects that are tested.

The current status of early foreign language instruction in the United States is bleak, with a decline over the past decade of 9 percentage points (from 24% to 15%) in the percentage of public elementary schools teaching foreign languages. This decline seems likely to continue given the number of districts that reported cutting back on foreign language programs for funding reasons. In addition, of the public elementary schools still teaching foreign languages, the percentage that offer only introductory or exploratory classes rather than a program aimed at achieving proficiency has kept steady at approximately half of all programs. This means that many of those elementary students who are receiving foreign language instruction are not being offered the opportunity to achieve any measure of proficiency. We therefore continue to urge school districts across the country to initiate comprehensive language programs with the aim of offering students the opportunity to develop high-level language skills over an extended period.

Recommendation 2

Offer more intensive foreign language programs.

Research has shown that intensive language instruction leads to better language proficiency outcomes (Johnson & Swain, 1997). In order for our nation's youth to develop the skills needed for global communication in the 21st century, our schools need to provide them with intensive language and cultural training. Despite increases over the past decade in the percentage of secondary schools offering Advanced Placement courses, language for native speakers classes, and International Baccalaureate classes, there has not been a major increase in intensive language programs.

The most common type of public elementary school foreign language program in 2008, offered by 44% of schools with language programs, was the exploratory model, which provides only introductory exposure to the language. The immersion model—the only model that consistently provides instruction that allows students to attain a high level of proficiency—was offered by only 6% of public schools with language programs. School districts across the country need to provide more options for both elementary and secondary students, including immersion-type foreign language programs, where selected academic subjects are taught in the foreign language.

Schools also need to reconsider the traditional method of measuring success in language learning, namely, "seat time," or the number of years a student has studied a language. This method has not proven to be successful because of wide variations in teaching methods and in students' language learning abilities. The profession now recognizes that standards that define what students should know and be able to do provide states and districts with a gauge for measuring student achievement and excellence in language curricula. The use of standards coupled with a focus on proficiency-based instruction (in contrast to previous methods such as grammar-translation and audio-lingual) will help students become successful users of the language they are learning—able to create and negotiate meaning on a variety of topics and to behave in culturally appropriate ways. The outcomes of these standards-based, proficiency-focused programs are well worth the effort: high student foreign language proficiency, enhanced academic success in English and other subject areas, and the ability to communicate and compete in an increasingly global workplace and community (Curtain & Dahlberg, 2004).

We recommend that school districts around the country, in collaboration with universities, educational associations, and research organizations, design and implement language programs that offer intensive, standards- and proficiency-based instruction from elementary school through high school.

Recommendation 3

Improve the articulation pattern for schools that offer foreign language classes in the early and middle school grades.

Between 1987 and 1997, no progress was seen in this area. Well-planned articulation of language programs from one level of schooling to the next continues to be a major challenge confronting the field at all levels, but the past decade has seen some positive growth at the high school level. More high schools in 2008 reported placing students with prior language experience in advanced classes where the course content and objectives were designed to provide continuity from their previous instruction. There are still many school districts with no sequencing plan to ensure smooth continuation of foreign language study from one level to the next, but more districts are starting to address this issue. We recommend that all school districts offering foreign language instruction adopt a coherent sequencing plan from elementary school through high school to ensure that every year, students are provided with foreign language instruction that builds on the knowledge and skills they have acquired in previous classes. This type of articulation is a necessity for students to achieve proficiency in the language they are studying.

Recommendation 4

Offer programs that teach major world languages.

Survey results over the years have revealed ups and downs in the teaching of specific languages. These variations sometimes appear to be politically motivated; schools change the languages they offer according to major world events and contexts. So, for example, the teaching of Russian saw an increase in the 1980s, Japanese rose in the 1990s, and Chinese and Arabic are on the rise now.

Our schools need to offer a wide range of languages, with instruction in each language available at multiple levels, so that students can develop a high level of proficiency over an extended period of time. The specific language taught is less important than the type and length of instruction offered. Development of a citizenry with proficiency in a wide range of languages will provide the United States with the linguistic

We recommend that school districts design and implement language programs that offer intensive, standards- and proficiency-based instruction from elementary school through high school.

and cultural skills needed to further international cooperation, national security, and commerce, among other areas.

We recommend that school districts implement strong programs in languages that make sense for their local context (e.g., availability of qualified teachers, presence of heritage language groups, proximity to or commerce with other countries) and that they maintain those programs through whatever international challenges arise. School districts cannot be expected to change the languages they offer at the whim of international events. If a district chooses to begin a program in a new language, we encourage them to add the new language to their existing repertoire without displacing any of the languages already offered.

Recommendation 5

Address the major problems identified by the survey, including insufficient funding, inequities in access to foreign language instruction, teacher shortages, and lack of certification among many elementary school language teachers.

Survey results showed that over the past decade, education priorities in the United States have not been focused on expanding the global skills of our nation's youth. Insufficient funding for language programs continues to be a major obstacle to the development of high-quality, long-sequence, well-articulated foreign language programs that allow students to achieve communicative proficiency. Compounding the problem is inequity in access to foreign language instruction: Rural schools and low SES schools were less likely than other schools to offer foreign languages to their students. A shortage of qualified language teachers also limits schools' ability to offer language instruction and has forced many districts to look for alternative sources of teachers. Survey results regarding teacher certification indicated a clear need for more teachers with certification in foreign language teaching at the elementary school level.

The implications for teacher training institutions are obvious, particularly in view of a national shortage of qualified language teachers (Long, 2004; Olsen, 2004). Universities and colleges need to expand their elementary school language teacher education programs and actively recruit foreign language teacher candidates (Long, 2004). At the same time, school districts, state departments of education, and the federal government need to revisit their educational priorities and identify ways to provide sufficient funding to meet the need for expanded language teacher education, certification, and professional development.

Recommendation 6

Expand the research base on foreign language instruction.

One necessary component of K–12 language education whose scarcity became more obvious as the survey progressed is quantitative and qualitative research on language instruction. For example, survey responses, especially from elementary schools, revealed a wide range of interpretations as to how much language instruction is needed to reach a certain degree of proficiency. Survey results also suggested a need for more data on the proficiency levels attained by secondary school students. This may be a good time for the profession to revisit the development and administration of a National Assessment of Educational Progress (NAEP), known as "the nation's report card," in foreign languages. Results would provide the nation with much needed data from a nationally representative assessment on what students know and can do in the foreign languages they have studied.

Research is clearly needed on proficiency outcomes in various types of language programs and with various language teaching methodologies. Researchers should also investigate what characterizes "good" language teaching and how teachers can maximize classroom time for the best proficiency results. Further study is also warranted to determine how technologies are being used in the language classroom and how effectively, to what extent, by whom, and for what purposes. Despite the sizeable increase in the use of technology in language instruction, we still know little about how technology-based materials are being used and to what extent they enhance foreign language learning.

Elevating the Importance of Language Education

More than 20 years after CAL first offered recommendations 1 through 5 above, we need to ask ourselves why significant progress has not been made on these issues, leaving the status of foreign language education in the United States relatively unchanged. We believe that the underlying cause is a widespread lack of recognition among policy makers of the importance of the ability to communicate in other languages and across cultures. Having more Americans with this ability would contribute greatly to our nation's capacity to maintain national security, promote international cooperation, and compete effectively in a global economy. We therefore offer the following recommendation, without which the others may be of no use:

Recognize the vital importance of an American citizenry that can communicate effectively in many languages and across cultures, and make the teaching and learning of foreign languages a priority in the K–12 curriculum.

Until there is widespread recognition that knowing another language is as important as knowing science, social studies, language arts, and mathematics, our ongoing recommendations are not likely to be implemented on a large scale. But if legislators, administrators, and other education policy makers recognize the need to incorporate foreign languages into the core curriculum, the necessary funding and other resources needed to make that happen will follow. This change in attitude is the necessary first step in moving our country toward parity with nations around the globe that graduate students who can communicate in more than one language.

Concluding Words

In his address to a joint session of Congress on February 24, 2009, President Barack Obama (2009) warned, "Our children will compete for jobs in a global economy that too many of our schools do not prepare them for." He announced that "the goal of this administration [is] to ensure that every child has access to a complete and competitive education—from the day they are born to the day they begin a career." In earlier speeches, Obama stated that "we should be emphasizing foreign languages in our schools from an early age" (Miller, 2008) and that he wants to ensure that "children are getting foreign languages, because this world is becoming more interdependent [and we need] to communicate across boundaries, across borders, and that's something frankly where we've fallen behind" (Sweet, 2008). We hope that the United States, through federal, state, and district-wide initiatives in the decade to come, can change the trajectory of language education documented in this survey and turn President Obama's vision into reality with an educational system that provides a world-class education to all children.

References

REFERENCES

American Council on the Teaching of Foreign Languages. (2002). *Program standards for the preparation of foreign language teachers.* Alexandria, VA: Author. Retrieved June 12, 2009, from http://www.actfl.org/files/public/ACTFLNCATEStandardsRevised713.pdf

American Council on the Teaching of Foreign Languages. (2007). *Foreign language in U.S. schools: National K-12 enrollments and project status.* Unpublished handout at ACTFL 2007 Annual Convention and World Languages Expo, San Antonio, TX.

American Council on the Teaching of Foreign Languages. (n.d.) *What the research says.* Retrieved September 4, 2009, from http://www.actfl.org/i4a/pages/Index.cfm?pageID=4524

Assembly Committee on Education. (2006, March). *Teacher credentialing: Subject matter knowledge: foreign languages.* [California] Assembly Bill 2054. Retrieved September 4, 2009, from http://info.sen.ca.gov/pub/05-06/bill/asm/ab_2051-2100/ab_2054_cfa_20060328_145159_asm_comm.html

Atkins, M., Supahan, S., & Lewis, C. (2008, April). *Fighting for validation: California indigenous language teacher credentialing.* Workshop presented at the Language in Life Conference, Sausalito, CA. Retrieved September 4, 2009, from http://www.aicls.org/pdf/LILC08Teacher_Sum.pdf

Bousquet, M. J. (1999). *Professional associations as recruiters: California's innovative approach to remedying the foreign language teacher shortage.* Stanford, CA: Stanford University, California Foreign Language Project. Retrieved August 7, 2009, from http://www.stanford.edu/group/CFLP/research/pareval/parevalindex.html

A call to action for national foreign language capabilities. (2005). Washington, DC: U.S. Department of Defense. Retrieved September 4, 2009, from http://www.eric.ed.gov/ERICDocs/data/ericdocs2sql/content_storage_01/0000019b/80/1b/b7/f3.pdf

Carter, G. R. (2008, January). Is it good for the kids? Making the grade in a global economy. *ASCD, News and Media.* Retrieved April 30, 2009, from http://www.ascd.org/news_media/Is_It_Good_for_the_Kids_Editorials/Is_It_Good_for_the_Kids_-_January_2008.aspx

College Board. (2009). *The fifth annual AP report to the nation: Subject-specific results.* Retrieved April 30, 2009, from http://www.collegeboard.com/html/aprtn/subject_specific_data.html

Committee for Economic Development (2006). *Education for global leadership: The importance of international studies and foreign language education for U.S. economic and national security.* Washington, DC: Author. Retrieved September 4, 2009, from http://www.ced.org/images/library/reports/education/report_foreignlanguages.pdf

Curtain, H., & Dahlberg, C. A. (2004). *Languages and children: Making the match. New languages for young learners, Grades K-8* (3rd ed.). Boston: Pearson.

Eddy, P. (1998). Foreign language needs of the federal government: Implications for early learning programs. In M. Met (Ed.), *Critical issues in early second language learning: Building for our children's future* (pp. 88-92). Glenview, IL: Scott Foresman-Addison Wesley.

Education, Audiovisual and Culture Executive Agency (EACEA P9 Eurydice). (2008). *Key data on teaching languages at school in Europe.* Brussels, Belgium: Author. Retrieved September 4, 2009, from http://epp.eurostat.ec.europa.eu/cache/ITY_OFFPUB/978-92-9201-003-4/EN/978-92-9201-003-4-EN.PDF

Ellis, R. (2008). *Principles of instructed second language acquisition.* Washington, DC: Center for Applied Linguistics. Retrieved August 13, 2009, from http://www.cal.org/resources/digest/instructed2ndlang.html

Furman, N., Goldberg, D., & Lusin, N. (2007). *Enrollments in languages other than English in United States institutions of higher education, Fall 2006.* New York: Modern Language Association. Retrieved April 30, 2009, from http://www.mla.org/2006_flenrollmentsurvey

Goals 2000: Educate America Act of 1994. Pub. L. No. 103-227, § 102 (1994). Retrieved September 4, 2009, from http://www.ed.gov/legislation/GOALS2000/TheAct/index.html

Grandin, J. M. (2001). *Why learn another language if the whole world speaks English?* Paper presented at the Rhode Island Foreign Language Association. Retrieved September 16, 2009, from http://www.dickinson.edu/prorg/nectfl/grandinspeech.html

Grandin, J. M. (2006). Globalization and its implications for the profession. In A.L. Heining-Boynton (Ed.), *ACTFL 2005-2015: Realizing our vision of languages for all* (pp.175-197). Upper Saddle River, NJ: Pearson.

Hammadou, J., & Bernhardt, E. (1987). On being and becoming a foreign language teacher. *Theory Into Practice, 26*(4), 301-306.

Heining-Boynton, A. L. (1990). Using FLES history to plan for the present and future. *Foreign Language Annals, 23*(6), 503-509.

Jackson, F. H., & Malone, M. E. (2009). *Building the foreign language capacity we need: Toward a comprehensive strategy for a national language framework.* Washington, DC: Center for Applied Linguistics. Retrieved September 4, 2009, from http://www.cal.org/resources/languageframework.pdf

Johnson, R. K., & Swain, M. (1997). *Immersion education: International perspectives.* Cambridge, UK: Cambridge University Press.

Krashen, S. (1985). *The input hypothesis.* Harlow, Essex, UK: Longman.

Language Learning Center. (2008, Summer). *Mapping and enhancing language learning in Washington state. Taking a closer look at high schools that don't offer world languages* (MELL Policy Brief #2). Seattle, WA: University of Washington. Retrieved April 30, 2009, from http://depts.washington.edu/mellwa/Reports/MELL_policy_brief_02.pdf

LinguaFolio. (n.d.). Retrieved September 4, 2009, from http://www.doe.virginia.gov/linguafolio/participate.html

Long, S. S. (2004). *"Visions" of K-12 foreign language teacher recruitment in higher education.* Ames: Iowa State University National K-12 Foreign Language Resource Center, New Visions in Action Task Force on Teacher Recruitment and Retention. Retrieved October 20, 2009 from http://www.nflrc.iastate.edu/nva/newsite/docarch/trr/2000PR05.html

Marzo, K. K. (2008). Analysis finds time stolen from other subjects for math, reading. *Education Week, 27*(25), 6. Retrieved April 30, 2009, from http://www.edweek.org/ew/articles/2008/02/27/25cep.h27.html/h27.html?print=1

Miller, S. (2008, July 11). *Como se dice? Obama clarifies comments over foreign languages. ABC News.* Retrieved September 4, 2009, from http://blogs.abcnews.com/politicalradar/2008/07/como-se-dice-ob.html

Murphy, P., DeArmond, M., & Guin, K. (2003). A national crisis or localized problems? Getting perspective on the scope and scale of the teacher shortage. *Education Policy Analysis Archives, 11*(3). Retrieved August 13, 2009, from http://epaa.asu.edu/epaa/v11n23

National Capital Language Resource Center. (n.d.). *Portfolio assessment in the foreign language classroom.* Retrieved September 4, 2009, from http://www.nclrc.org/portfolio/index.html

National Center for Education Statistics. (1997). *Teacher professionalization and teacher commitment: A multilevel analysis.* Washington, DC: U.S. Department of Education. Retrieved June 8, 2009, from http://nces.ed.gov/pubs/97069.pdf

National Council of State Supervisors for Languages. (2009). *LinguaFolio.* Retrieved April 30, 2009, from http://www.ncssfl.org/links/index.php?linguafolio

National Standards in Foreign Language Education Project. (2006). *Standards for foreign language learning in the 21st century.* Lawrence, KS: Allen Press.

Obama, B. (2009, February 24). Speech presented to Joint Session of Congress, Washington, DC. Retrieved June 10, 2009, from www.whitehouse.gov/the_press_office/remarks-of-president-barack-obama-address-to-joint-session-of-congress/

Olsen, P. R. (2004, February 18.) Schools seek private firms to teach foreign tongues. *New York Times.* Retrieved October 20, 2009, from http://www.nytimes.com/2004/02/18/education/18outsource.html

Partnership for 21st Century Skills. (2007). *Beyond the three Rs: Voter attitudes toward 21st century skills.* Retrieved September 4, 2009, from http://www.21stcenturyskills.org/documents/P21_poll-report_singlepg.pdf

Partnership for 21st Century Skills. (2009). *Framework for 21st century learning.* Retrieved September 4, 2009, from http://www.21stcenturyskills.org/documents/framework_flyer_updated_april_2009.pdf

Pufahl, I., Rhodes, N. C., & Christian, D. (2000). *Foreign language teaching: What the United States can learn from other countries.* Washington, DC: Center for Applied Linguistics. Available from http://www.cal.org/resources/pubs/US_can_learn.html

Rhodes, N., & Gilzow, D. (2005, April 1). *Seven model early foreign language programs: Five years later.* Paper presented at the Northeast Conference on the Teaching of Foreign Languages, New York.

Rhodes, N. C., & Branaman, L. E. (1999). *Foreign language instruction in the United States: A national survey of elementary and secondary schools.* McHenry, IL, and Washington, DC: Delta Systems and Center for Applied Linguistics.

Rhodes, N. C., & Oxford, R. (1988). Foreign languages in elementary and secondary schools: Results of a national survey. *Foreign Language Annals, 21*(1), 51-69.

Rosenbusch, M. H., & Jensen, J. (2005). Status of foreign language programs in the NECTFL states. *NECTFL Review, 56,* 26-37.

Sadow, S. (1996). Career development for the language professional. *Foreign Language, 29*(2), 152-162.

Schrier, L. L. (2001). Developing precollegiate foreign language teachers: An overlooked mission of foreign language departments. *ADFL Bulletin, 32*(3), 71-78. Retrieved June 11, 2009, from http://web2.adfl.org/ADFL/bulletin/v32n3/323071.htm

Sweet, L. (2008, February 21). Complete transcript of Democratic debate. Austin, February 21, 2008. *Chicago Sun Times.* Retrieved April 30, 2009, from http://blogs.suntimes.com/sweet/2008/02/sweet_complete_transcript_of_d.html

Swender, E., & Duncan, G. (1998). ACTFL performance guidelines for K-12 learners. *Foreign Language Annals, 31*(4), 479-483.

Taboada, M. B. (2004, January 26). Leander mom brings Spanish to elementary school: Grass-roots efforts to teach foreign languages early are a national trend. *Austin American-Statesman*. Retrieved September 4, 2009, from http://www.spanish-forkids.com/leander.pdf

Talbert, J., & McLaughlin, M. (1993). Teacher professionalism in local school contexts. *American Journal of Education, 102*, 123–153.

U.S. Department of Education. (2008). *National Security Language Initiative (NSLI)*. Retrieved October 20, 2009, from http://www.ed.gov/about/inits/ed/competitiveness/nsli/about.html

Viadero, D. (1991, November 6). Foreign-language instruction resurfacing in elementary schools. *Education Week*. Retrieved September 4, 2009, from http://www.edweek.org/ew/articles/1991/11/06/10lang.h11.html?qa=Foreign-language_instruction_resurfacing_in_elementary_schools

Wilkerson, C. (2008). Instructors' use of English in the modern language classroom. *Foreign Language Annals, 41*(2), 310-320.

Appendixes

APPENDIX A

NATIONAL K–12 FOREIGN LANGUAGE SURVEY
Elementary School Questionnaire

To: School Principal or Foreign Language Teacher

This survey is about foreign language instruction in your school during the 2007–08 school year. Please complete the survey, *even if your school does not offer foreign language instruction.* In this survey, foreign language instruction refers to the teaching of any language(s) other than English. If your school teaches elementary through middle or high school levels, please fill out the survey only as it applies to the *elementary grades* at your school.

You can complete this survey online or by mail.

To complete the survey online: Go to www.cal.org/languagesurvey. Use the login ID and password on your address label below.

To complete the survey by mail: Fill out this survey and return it in the postage-paid envelope provided. Please correct any inaccurate information on the address label.

Please respond to the survey (online or by mail) by October 31, 2007. Thank you very much!

Questions: Contact Dr. Ingrid Pufahl at 202-355-1567 or by email at ingrid@cal.org.

Center for Applied Linguistics
4646 40th Street, NW
Washington, DC 20016-3740

Name of person filling out questionnaire: ______________________

Title/position: ______________________

Contact information (in case of questions): Telephone: ______________ **Email:** ______________

☐ **If you'd like a copy of the survey results, please check here and make sure you've included your email address above.**

1. What grades does your school include? *(Check all that apply)*

a. ☐ Prekindergarten
b. ☐ Kindergarten
c. ☐ Grade 1
d. ☐ Grade 2
e. ☐ Grade 3
f. ☐ Grade 4
g. ☐ Grade 5
h. ☐ Grade 6
i. ☐ Grade 7
j. ☐ Grade 8
k. ☐ Other *(specify)*: ______________

2. How many students currently attend your school?

________ Number of students

3. Does your school currently teach foreign language(s)?

☐1 Yes → SKIP TO QUESTION 5
☐2 No

4. Is your school planning to offer foreign language instruction in the next 2 years?

☐1 Yes ☐2 No

NOTE: *If your school does not teach foreign language(s), you do not need to complete any more of the survey. Please mail it back to us in the enclosed postage-paid envelope. Thank you for your help!*

5. How many of the students in your school are currently enrolled in foreign language classes?

________ Number of students

6. When are the classes taught? *(Check all that apply)*:

a. ☐ During the regular school day
b. ☐ Before or after school
c. ☐ Other *(specify)*: ______________

Center for Applied Linguistics & Westat
www.cal.org

Funded by the U.S. Department of Education, International Research and Studies Program

NATIONAL K–12 FOREIGN LANGUAGE SURVEY | Elementary School Questionnaire

Goals for foreign language program types		
Program Type A: Exploratory	**Program Type B: Language Focus**	**Program Type C: Immersion**
Goals: Gain general exposure to language and culture, learn basic words and phrases, and/or develop an interest in foreign language for future study. Portions of this program may be taught in English. (Often called *FLEX—foreign language experience/exploratory*)	**Goals:** Acquire listening, speaking, reading, and writing skills; gain an understanding of and appreciation for other cultures. Focus of instruction can be on language and/or subject content. (Often called *FLES—foreign language in the elementary school*)	**Goals:** Be able to communicate in the language with a high level of proficiency and acquire an understanding of and appreciation for other cultures. At least *50 percent of the school day* is taught in the foreign language, including academic subjects. (Called *partial, total,* or *two-way immersion,* depending on the amount of foreign language used and the make-up of the student body)

7. **In the chart below, mark each language taught at your school. For each of the languages taught, mark the *corresponding letter of the program type* from the three descriptions above that best describes your program, the *number of students in your school studying that language*, the *grades* in which it is offered, and an *average number of minutes per week* students spend in the study of the foreign language.** *Note: If you have more than one program type for a language, or if instruction time differs substantially by grade level, please indicate this under "Other."*

EXAMPLE:

Languages	Program Type A	B	C	Number of Students	PreK	K	1	2	3	4	5	6	7	8	Average Mins/Week
a. ☒ Arabic	☐	☒	☐	75	☒	☒	☒	☒	☒	☐	☐	☐	☐	☐	150 mins

Languages	Program Type A	B	C	Number of Students	PreK	K	1	2	3	4	5	6	7	8	Average Mins/Week
a. ☐ Arabic	☐	☐	☐	____	☐	☐	☐	☐	☐	☐	☐	☐	☐	☐	____
b. ☐ Chinese	☐	☐	☐	____	☐	☐	☐	☐	☐	☐	☐	☐	☐	☐	____
c. ☐ French	☐	☐	☐	____	☐	☐	☐	☐	☐	☐	☐	☐	☐	☐	____
d. ☐ German	☐	☐	☐	____	☐	☐	☐	☐	☐	☐	☐	☐	☐	☐	____
e. ☐ Hebrew	☐	☐	☐	____	☐	☐	☐	☐	☐	☐	☐	☐	☐	☐	____
f. ☐ Italian	☐	☐	☐	____	☐	☐	☐	☐	☐	☐	☐	☐	☐	☐	____
g. ☐ Japanese	☐	☐	☐	____	☐	☐	☐	☐	☐	☐	☐	☐	☐	☐	____
h. ☐ Latin	☐	☐	☐	____	☐	☐	☐	☐	☐	☐	☐	☐	☐	☐	____
i. ☐ Portuguese	☐	☐	☐	____	☐	☐	☐	☐	☐	☐	☐	☐	☐	☐	____
j. ☐ Russian	☐	☐	☐	____	☐	☐	☐	☐	☐	☐	☐	☐	☐	☐	____
k. ☐ Sign Language (American)	☐	☐	☐	____	☐	☐	☐	☐	☐	☐	☐	☐	☐	☐	____
l. ☐ Spanish	☐	☐	☐	____	☐	☐	☐	☐	☐	☐	☐	☐	☐	☐	____
Other *(Specify)*															
m. ☐ ____________	☐	☐	☐	____	☐	☐	☐	☐	☐	☐	☐	☐	☐	☐	____
n. ☐ ____________	☐	☐	☐	____	☐	☐	☐	☐	☐	☐	☐	☐	☐	☐	____
o. ☐ ____________	☐	☐	☐	____	☐	☐	☐	☐	☐	☐	☐	☐	☐	☐	____
Language for Native (or Heritage) Language Speakers															
p. ☐ Spanish for Spanish Speakers	☐	☐	☐	____	☐	☐	☐	☐	☐	☐	☐	☐	☐	☐	____
q. ☐ Other *(specify)*: ____________	☐	☐	☐	____	☐	☐	☐	☐	☐	☐	☐	☐	☐	☐	____

Page 2

8a. What percentage of your language classes last for the entire school year?

_____ Percent (If 100%, ⟶ SKIP TO QUESTION 9)

8b. For those language classes that do not last for the entire school year, please identify the average length of the classes. *(Check only one)*

- ☐₁ 1–5 weeks
- ☐₂ 6–10 weeks
- ☐₃ 11–15 weeks
- ☐₄ More than 15 weeks

9. How many foreign language teachers (full or part-time) are there in your school?

_____ Number of foreign language teachers

10. Please write in the number of foreign language teachers in your school who are certified for: *(Write one number for each line; if answer is none, write "0")*

a. ___ Elementary school teaching, but *not* specifically for foreign language teaching

b. ___ Foreign language teaching at the elementary school level

c. ___ Foreign language teaching at the elementary school level *and* for elementary school teaching

d. ___ Foreign language teaching at the K–12 level

e. ___ Foreign language teaching at the *secondary school* level but *not* at the elementary level

f. ___ Others who are *not* certified (e.g., paraprofessionals, career changers, volunteers, college students)

11. Please write in the number of foreign language teachers in your school who are native speakers of the language they teach. *(If the answer is none, write "0")*

_____ Number of native-speaking foreign language teachers

12. Are any of your foreign language teachers hired through alternative means (e.g., agencies that provide teachers from other countries, commercial language schools, foreign governments)?

☐₁ Yes ☐₂ No

If yes, please explain: ________________________________

____

13. Have any of the foreign language teachers at your school participated in professional development or in-service teacher training in their subject area during the past 12 months?

☐₁ Yes ☐₂ No

14. To what extent do language teachers in your school use the foreign language in the classroom? If you have more than one language program model, please answer for the program that sets the highest proficiency goals. *(Check only one)*

- ☐₁ Less than 50% of the time
- ☐₂ 50–74% of the time
- ☐₃ 75–90% of the time
- ☐₄ More than 90% of the time

15. Is there an established and written foreign language curriculum or set of guidelines for your program(s)?

☐₁ Yes ☐₂ No

16. How often do foreign language teachers in your school use the following instructional materials? (*Please indicate, for each type, whether it is used* frequently, sometimes, *or* not at all)

	Frequently	Sometimes	Not at all
a. Commercially published textbooks/workbooks	☐₁	☐₂	☐₃
b. Teacher-made materials *(specify)*: ________________	☐₁	☐₂	☐₃
c. Literature from the target culture (e.g., stories, books, songs, poems/rhymes)	☐₁	☐₂	☐₃
d. Media (e.g., films, videotapes, DVDs, CDs, audiotapes)	☐₁	☐₂	☐₃
e. Authentic materials from the target culture (realia) (e.g., menus, magazines, advertisements, newspapers, bus tickets)	☐₁	☐₂	☐₃
f. Visual/tactile materials (e.g., puppets, posters, pictures, flash cards, games, puzzles)	☐₁	☐₂	☐₃
g. Internet resources (e.g., World Wide Web, online activities, virtual tours, electronic mail, discussion lists, chats, blogs, wikis, podcasts)	☐₁	☐₂	☐₃
h. Computer-assisted instructional materials (e.g., computer software programs, CD-ROMs)	☐₁	☐₂	☐₃
i. Other instructional technology (e.g., satellite broadcasts, interactive television, video conferencing)	☐₁	☐₂	☐₃
j. Other *(specify)*: ________________	☐₁	☐₂	☐₃

NATIONAL K–12 FOREIGN LANGUAGE SURVEY | Elementary School Questionnaire

17. How is students' foreign language proficiency assessed at your school? *(For each assessment format listed, please indicate whether it is used* frequently, sometimes, *or* not at all)

	Frequently	Sometimes	Not at all
a. Student use of illustrations to indicate comprehension (e.g., match illustrations to sequence heard or read)	☐1	☐2	☐3
b. Student use of English (or native language) to explain what is understood from something heard, read, or viewed in the target language	☐1	☐2	☐3
c. Oral proficiency interviews (teacher or outside evaluator interviews individual student to determine student's fluency)	☐1	☐2	☐3
d. Student presentations (e.g., student prepares presentation/demonstration and delivers it to demonstrate proficiency in the foreign language)	☐1	☐2	☐3
e. Oral language activities (e.g., student conducts interview, describes drawing, engages in interpersonal exchange or impromptu skit)	☐1	☐2	☐3
f. Written works produced by student (essays, letters, reports, brochures)	☐1	☐2	☐3
g. Student portfolios (e.g., compilation of student-selected and/or teacher-selected work over a set period of time, with rating criteria)	☐1	☐2	☐3
h. Student self-assessment (e.g., student evaluates his/her language skills using oral/written self-evaluations)	☐1	☐2	☐3
i. Translation exercises (e.g., English → German; German → English)	☐1	☐2	☐3
j. Selected-response tests (e.g., multiple choice or matching of vocabulary words or grammar structures)	☐1	☐2	☐3
k. Short-answer tests (student is asked to respond in writing to questions)	☐1	☐2	☐3
l. Other (e.g., standardized tests) *(please describe)*: ______	☐1	☐2	☐3

18. Do the foreign language teachers at your school routinely integrate the National Standards for Foreign Language Learning and/or state foreign language standards into their instruction?

☐1 Yes ☐2 No

Optional comments: ______________________

19. What type of sequencing (articulation) exists for students who have studied foreign language(s) at your school when they continue to junior high/middle school? *(Mark the one statement below that best describes the sequencing for the majority of the students at your school)*

☐1 Students are placed in exploratory language classes (general exposure to one or more languages and cultures)

☐2 Students are placed in Level I foreign language classes along with students who have had no prior instruction in the language

☐3 Students are placed in more advanced classes where the course content and objectives are designed specifically to provide continuity from their prior level

☐4 Students are placed in more advanced classes where the course content and objectives are *not* designed specifically to provide continuity from their prior level

☐5 Students can enroll in some subject matter courses taught in the foreign language

☐6 There is no foreign language instruction (for the language(s) taught in our elementary school) in junior high/middle school in our district

☐7 Other *(specify)*: ______________________

20. Has foreign language instruction in your school been affected by a shortage of qualified language teachers?

☐1 Yes ☐2 No

If yes, please explain *how* foreign language instruction has been affected by the shortage: ______________________

21. Has foreign language instruction in your school been affected by No Child Left Behind legislation?

☐1 Yes ☐2 No

If yes, please explain: ______________________

Please include any additional comments/questions here or on a separate sheet.

PLEASE RETURN THIS SURVEY *BY OCTOBER 31, 2007,* IN THE ENCLOSED POSTAGE-PAID ENVELOPE.

Thank you very much for completing this survey!

Center for Applied Linguistics
4646 40th Street, NW
Washington, DC 20016-3740

National K–12 Foreign Language Survey – Center for Applied Linguistics & Westat

Page 4

APPENDIX B

NATIONAL K–12 FOREIGN LANGUAGE SURVEY
Middle School/Junior High and High School Questionnaire

To: Foreign Language Chairperson or Foreign Language Teacher

This survey is about foreign language instruction in your school during the 2007–08 school year. Please complete the survey, *even if your school does not offer foreign language instruction.* In this survey, foreign language instruction refers to the teaching of any language(s) other than English. If your school teaches elementary through middle or high school levels, please fill out the survey only as it applies to the *middle school/junior high and/or high school grades* at your school.

You can complete this survey online or by mail.

To complete the survey online: Go to www.cal.org/languagesurvey. Use the login ID and password on your address label below.

To complete the survey by mail: Fill out this survey and return it in the postage-paid envelope provided. Please correct any inaccurate information on the address label.

Please respond to the survey (online or by mail) by October 31, 2007. Thank you very much!

Questions: Contact Dr. Ingrid Pufahl at 202-355-1567 or by email at ingrid@cal.org.

Center for Applied Linguistics
4646 40th Street, NW
Washington, DC 20016-3740

Name of person filling out questionnaire: ____________

Title/position: ____________

Contact information (in case of questions): Telephone: ____________ **Email:** ____________

☐ **If you'd like a copy of the survey results, please check here and make sure you've included your email address above.**

1. **What grades does your school include?**
   (Check all that apply)
   - a. ☐ Grade 5
   - b. ☐ Grade 6
   - c. ☐ Grade 7
   - d. ☐ Grade 8
   - e. ☐ Grade 9
   - f. ☐ Grade 10
   - g. ☐ Grade 11
   - h. ☐ Grade 12
   - i. ☐ Other *(specify)*: ____________

2. **How many students currently attend your school?**

   ________ Number of students

3. **Does your school currently teach foreign language(s)?**

   ☐ 1 Yes → SKIP TO QUESTION 5
   ☐ 2 No

4. **Is your school planning to offer foreign language instruction in the next 2 years?**

   ☐ 1 Yes ☐ 2 No

***NOTE:** If your school does not teach foreign language(s), you do not need to complete any more of the survey. Please mail it back to us in the enclosed postage-paid envelope. Thank you for your help!*

5. **How many of the students in your school are currently enrolled in foreign language classes?**

   ________ Number of students

CAL CENTER FOR APPLIED LINGUISTICS

Center for Applied Linguistics & Westat
www.cal.org

WESTAT

Funded by the U.S. Department of Education, International Research and Studies Program

NATIONAL K–12 FOREIGN LANGUAGE SURVEY | Middle/High School Questionnaire

6. In the chart below, mark each language taught at your school, the *levels* offered, the *average number of hours per week* spent in the foreign language class, and the approximate *number of students* in your school currently studying that language.

EXAMPLE: Languages	Level 1 2 3 4 5 6	Average Hours/Week	Number of Students
a. ☒ Arabic	☒ ☒ ☐ ☐ ☐ ☐	5	45

Languages	Level 1 2 3 4 5 6	Average Hours/Week	Number of Students
a. ☐ Arabic	☐ ☐ ☐ ☐ ☐ ☐	____	____
b. ☐ Chinese	☐ ☐ ☐ ☐ ☐ ☐	____	____
c. ☐ French	☐ ☐ ☐ ☐ ☐ ☐	____	____
d. ☐ German	☐ ☐ ☐ ☐ ☐ ☐	____	____
e. ☐ Hebrew	☐ ☐ ☐ ☐ ☐ ☐	____	____
f. ☐ Italian	☐ ☐ ☐ ☐ ☐ ☐	____	____
g. ☐ Japanese	☐ ☐ ☐ ☐ ☐ ☐	____	____
h. ☐ Latin	☐ ☐ ☐ ☐ ☐ ☐	____	____
i. ☐ Portuguese	☐ ☐ ☐ ☐ ☐ ☐	____	____
j. ☐ Russian	☐ ☐ ☐ ☐ ☐ ☐	____	____
k. ☐ Sign Language (American)	☐ ☐ ☐ ☐ ☐ ☐	____	____
l. ☐ Spanish	☐ ☐ ☐ ☐ ☐ ☐	____	____
Other *(Specify)*			
m. ☐ ________	☐ ☐ ☐ ☐ ☐ ☐	____	____
n. ☐ ________	☐ ☐ ☐ ☐ ☐ ☐	____	____
o. ☐ ________	☐ ☐ ☐ ☐ ☐ ☐	____	____
Language for native (or heritage) language speakers	1 2 3 4 5 6		
p. ☐ Spanish for Spanish Speakers	☐ ☐ ☐ ☐ ☐ ☐	____	____
q. ☐ Other *(specify)*: ________	☐ ☐ ☐ ☐ ☐ ☐	____	____
Exploratory programs			
r. ☐ Exploratory French		____	____
s. ☐ Exploratory German		____	____
t. ☐ Exploratory Japanese		____	____
u. ☐ Exploratory Spanish		____	____
v. ☐ Other *(specify)*: ________		____	____

7a. What percentage of your language classes last for the entire school year?

_____ Percent (If 100% ⟶ SKIP TO QUESTION 8)

7b. For those language classes that do not last for the entire school year, please identify the average length of the classes. *(Check only one)*

- ☐1 1–5 weeks
- ☐2 6–10 weeks
- ☐3 11–15 weeks
- ☐4 More than 15 weeks

8. What types of foreign language classes are offered at your school? *(Please check each type offered)*

- a. ☐ Standard (listening, speaking, reading, writing, and culture)
- b. ☐ Exploratory (general exposure to one or more languages and cultures)
- c. ☐ Literature only
- d. ☐ Conversation only
- e. ☐ Advanced Placement (for college credit)
- f. ☐ Honors/Accelerated (other than Advanced Placement)
- g. ☐ International Baccalaureate (IB)
- h. ☐ Language for native or heritage language speakers (e.g., Spanish for Spanish speakers) *(specify languages)*: ____________
- i. ☐ Regular subjects (e.g., history, math, science) taught *in* the foreign language *(specify language and subject)*: ____________
- j. ☐ Distance learning (classes taught via distance technology) *(specify languages and delivery of format)*: ____________
- k. ☐ Other *(please specify)*: ____________

9. How many foreign language teachers (full- or part-time) are there in your school?

_____ Number of foreign language teachers

10. Please write in the number of foreign language teachers (full- and/or part-time) in your school who are certified for: *(Write one number for each line; if answer is none, write "0")*

- a. ____ Foreign language teaching at the secondary school level
- b. ____ Foreign language teaching at the K–12 level
- c. ____ Secondary school teaching but *not* specifically foreign language teaching
- d. ____ Foreign language teaching at the elementary school level but not at the secondary level
- e. ____ A different foreign language from the one they teach
- f. ____ More than one foreign language
- g. ____ Recognized as National Board Certified
- h. ____ Others who are not certified (e.g., paraprofessionals, career changers, volunteers, college students)

Page 2

11. Please write in the number of foreign language teachers in your school who are native speakers of the language they teach. *(If the answer is none, write "0")*

_______ Number of native-speaking foreign language teachers

12. Have any of the foreign language teachers at your school participated in professional development or in-service teacher training in their subject area during the past 12 months?

☐ 1 Yes ☐ 2 No

13. To what extent do language teachers in your school use the foreign language in the classroom? *(Check only one)*

☐ 1 Less than 50% of the time
☐ 2 50–74% of the time
☐ 3 75–90% of the time
☐ 4 More than 90% of the time

Comments: ______________________________

____

____

____

14. Is there an established and written foreign language curriculum or set of guidelines for your program(s)?

☐ 1 Yes ☐ 2 No

15. Do the foreign language teachers at your school routinely integrate the National Standards for Foreign Language Learning and/or state foreign language standards into their instruction?

☐ 1 Yes ☐ 2 No

Optional comments: ______________________________

____

____

____

____

16. How often do foreign language teachers in your school use the following instructional materials? (*Please indicate, for each type, whether it is used* frequently, sometimes, *or* not at all)

	Frequently	Sometimes	Not at all
a. Commercially published textbooks/ workbooks	☐ 1	☐ 2	☐ 3
b. Teacher-made materials *(specify)*: ______________________ ______________________	☐ 1	☐ 2	☐ 3
c. Literature from the target culture (e.g., stories, books, songs, poems)	☐ 1	☐ 2	☐ 3
d. Media (e.g., films, videotapes, DVDs, CDs, audiotapes)	☐ 1	☐ 2	☐ 3
e. Authentic materials from the target culture (realia) (e.g., menus, magazines, advertisements, newspapers, bus tickets, movie posters)	☐ 1	☐ 2	☐ 3
f. Visual/tactile materials (e.g., posters, pictures, flash cards, games, puzzles)	☐ 1	☐ 2	☐ 3
g. Internet resources (e.g., World Wide Web, Web Quests, online activities, virtual tours, electronic mail, discussion lists, chats, blogs, wikis, podcasts)	☐ 1	☐ 2	☐ 3
h. Computer-assisted instructional materials (e.g., computer software programs, CD-ROMs)	☐ 1	☐ 2	☐ 3
i. Other instructional technology (e.g., satellite broadcasts, interactive television, video conferencing)	☐ 1	☐ 2	☐ 3
j. Other *(specify)*: ______________________	☐ 1	☐ 2	☐ 3

NATIONAL K–12 FOREIGN LANGUAGE SURVEY | Middle/High School Questionnaire

17. How is students' foreign language proficiency assessed at your school? *(For each assessment format listed, please indicate whether it is used* frequently, sometimes, *or* not at all)

	Frequently	*Sometimes*	*Not at all*
a. Student use of illustrations to indicate comprehension (e.g., match illustrations to sequence heard or read)	☐1	☐2	☐3
b. Student use of English (or native language) to explain what is understood from something heard, read, or viewed in the target language	☐1	☐2	☐3
c. Oral proficiency interviews (teacher or outside evaluator interviews individual student to determine student's fluency)	☐1	☐2	☐3
d. Student presentations (e.g., student prepares presentation/demonstration and delivers it to demonstrate proficiency in the foreign language)	☐1	☐2	☐3
e. Oral language activities (e.g., student conducts interview, describes drawing, engages in interpersonal exchange or impromptu skit)	☐1	☐2	☐3
f. Written works produced by student (essays, letters, reports, brochures)	☐1	☐2	☐3
g. Student portfolios (e.g., compilation of student-selected and/or teacher-selected work over a set period of time, with rating criteria)	☐1	☐2	☐3
h. Student self-assessment (e.g., student evaluates his/her language skills using oral/written self-evaluations)	☐1	☐2	☐3
i. Translation exercises (e.g., English → German; German → English)	☐1	☐2	☐3
j. Selected-response tests (e.g., multiple choice or matching of vocabulary words or grammar structures)	☐1	☐2	☐3
k. Short-answer tests (student is asked to respond in writing to questions)	☐1	☐2	☐3
l. Standardized exams (e.g., AP exams, National German Examination, National Latin Exam, National Spanish Exam, SAT II, STAMP) *(specify)*: ____________	☐1	☐2	☐3
m. Other (please describe): ____________	☐1	☐2	☐3

18. What type of sequencing (articulation) exists for students who have studied foreign language(s) at their previous school level (i.e., in elementary school or middle/junior high school) when they continue foreign language study in your school? *(Mark the one statement below that best describes the sequencing for the majority of the students at your school)*

- ☐1 Students in our school district do not have foreign language instruction (in the language(s) we teach) before they enter our school
- ☐2 Students are placed in exploratory language classes (general exposure to one or more languages and cultures)
- ☐3 Students are placed in Level I foreign language classes along with students who have had no prior instruction in the language
- ☐4 Students are placed in more advanced classes where the course content and objectives are designed specifically to provide continuity from their prior level
- ☐5 Students are placed in more advanced classes where the course content and objectives are *not* designed specifically to provide continuity from their prior level
- ☐6 Students can enroll in some subject matter courses taught in the foreign language
- ☐7 Other *(specify)*: ____________

19. Has foreign language instruction in your school been affected by a shortage of qualified language teachers?

☐1 Yes ☐2 No

If yes, please explain *how* foreign language instruction has been affected by the shortage: ____________

20. Has foreign language instruction in your school been affected by No Child Left Behind legislation?

☐1 Yes ☐2 No

If yes, please explain: ____________

Please include any additional comments/questions here or on a separate sheet.

PLEASE RETURN THIS SURVEY *BY OCTOBER 31, 2007,* IN THE ENCLOSED POSTAGE-PAID ENVELOPE.

Thank you very much for completing this survey!

Center for Applied Linguistics
4646 40th Street, NW
Washington, DC 20016-3740

National K–12 Foreign Language Survey – Center for Applied Linguistics & Westat

Page 4

APPENDIX C
Foreign Language Conference Regions as of 2008

Central States (16)

Arkansas, Illinois, Indiana, Iowa, Kansas, **Kentucky**, Michigan, Minnesota, Missouri, Nebraska, North Dakota, Ohio, **Oklahoma**, South Dakota, **Tennessee**, and Wisconsin

Northeast (12)

Connecticut, Delaware, District of Columbia, Maine, Maryland, Massachusetts, New Hampshire, New Jersey, New York, Pennsylvania, Rhode Island, and Vermont

Pacific Northwest (6)

Alaska, Idaho, Montana, Oregon, Washington, and Wyoming

Southern (9)

Alabama, Florida, Georgia, Louisiana, Mississippi, North Carolina, South Carolina, **Virginia,** and **West Virginia**

Southwest (8)

Arizona, California, **Colorado,** Hawaii, Nevada, New Mexico, **Texas**, and Utah

Note: The 8 states in **bold** (Arkansas, Colorado, Kentucky, Oklahoma, Tennessee, Texas, Virginia, and West Virginia) are considered to be part of more than one region. For the purpose of this survey, they are included in only one region. California and Hawaii were part of the Pacific Northwest region in the 1997 survey, but they are now included in the Southwest.

Full Names of Conference Regions

Central States Conference on the Teaching of Foreign Languages (CSC)

Northeast Conference on the Teaching of Foreign Languages (NEC)

Pacific Northwest Council for Languages (PNCFL)

Southern Conference on Language Teaching (SCOLT)

Southwest Conference on Language Teaching (SWCOLT)

APPENDIX D
Tables for Standard Error and Statistical Significance

List of Tables

Note: Statistically significant differences are indicated with an asterisk (*), which means that the differences obtained are unlikely to have occurred by chance. The significance level used for these data is 0.05, noted as $p<0.05$, which means that there is less than a 5% probability (p) that the difference between two numbers presented happened only by chance.

Table A. Differences by School Level and School Type in the Percentage of Schools Offering Foreign Languages in 2008 and 1997

	2008		1997					
	x(1)	SE x(1)	x(2)	SE x(2)	x(1) - x(2)	Standard error of the difference	*t*	Significant ($p < .05$)
Elementary, total	25.2	0.81	31.1	1.46	-5.900	1.67	-3.53	* (decrease)
Public	14.7	0.91	29.8	1.68	-15.100	1.91	-7.90	* (decrease)
Private	51.2	2.07	52.6	3.12	-1.400	3.74	-0.37	
Secondary, total	78.8	1.55	85.8	0.99	-7.000	1.84	-3.81	* (decrease)
Public	76.4	1.81	85.1	1.08	-8.700	2.11	-4.13	* (decrease)
Private	88.2	1.64	91.7	2.21	-3.500	2.75	-1.27	

Table B. Differences by Metro Status in the Percentage of Public and Private Elementary Schools Offering Foreign Languages in 2008

	Public		Private					
	x(1)	SE x(1)	x(2)	SE x(2)	x(1) - x(2)	Standard error of the difference	*t*	Significant ($p < .05$)
Urban	15.1	1.97	57.1	3.48	-42.000	4.00	-10.50	*(difference)
Suburban	18.3	1.41	62.7	3.19	-44.400	3.49	-12.73	*(difference)
Rural	11.4	1.63	29.4	3.79	-18.000	4.13	-4.36	*(difference)

Table C. Differences by Metro Status, School Size, Region, and Socioeconomic Status in the Percentage of Elementary Schools Offering Foreign Languages in 2008

	x(1)	SE x(1)	x(2)	SE x(2)	x(1) - x(2)	Standard error of the difference	*t*	Significant ($p < .05$)
Metro status								
Urban/Suburban	28.6	1.72	32.3	1.43	-3.700	2.24	-1.65	
Urban/Rural	28.6	1.72	15.6	1.51	13.000	2.29	5.68	*(difference)
Suburban/Rural	32.3	1.43	15.6	1.51	16.700	2.08	8.03	*(difference)
School size								
<400/400-699	30.9	1.37	17.6	1.22	13.300	1.83	7.25	*(difference)
<400/700-999	30.9	1.37	19.4	2.05	11.500	2.47	4.66	*(difference)
<400/>1,000	30.9	1.37	20.5	4.77	10.400	4.96	2.10	*(difference)
400-699/700-999	17.6	1.22	19.4	2.05	-1.800	2.39	-0.75	
400-699/>1,000	17.6	1.22	20.5	4.77	-2.900	4.92	-0.59	
700-999/>1,000	19.4	2.05	20.5	4.77	-1.100	5.19	-0.21	
Region								
NEC/SCOLT	32.7	2.13	30.6	1.86	2.100	2.83	0.74	
NEC/SWCOLT	32.7	2.13	22.4	1.7	10.300	2.73	3.78	*(difference)
NEC/CSC	32.7	2.13	20.0	1.58	12.700	2.65	4.79	*(difference)
NEC/PNCFL	32.7	2.13	24.9	3.99	7.800	4.52	1.72	
SCOLT/SWCOLT	30.6	1.86	22.4	1.7	8.200	2.52	3.25	*(difference)
SCOLT/CSC	30.6	1.86	20.0	1.58	10.600	2.44	4.34	*(difference)
SCOLT/PNCFL	30.6	1.86	24.9	3.99	5.700	4.40	1.29	
SWCOLT/CSC	22.4	1.7	20.0	1.58	2.400	2.32	1.03	
SWCOLT/PNCFL	22.4	1.7	24.9	3.99	-2.500	4.34	-0.58	
CSC/PNCFL	20.0	1.58	24.9	3.99	-4.900	4.29	-1.14	
Socioeconomic status								
<20%/20%-39%[a]	21.5	2.32	11.0	1.74	10.500	2.90	3.62	*(difference)
<20%/40%-69%[a]	21.5	2.32	12.4	1.53	9.100	2.78	3.27	*(difference)
<20%/>70%[a]	21.5	2.32	14.1	1.91	7.400	3.01	2.46	*(difference)
20%-39%/40%-69%[a]	11.0	1.74	12.4	1.53	-1.400	2.32	-0.60	
20%-39%/>70%[a]	11.0	1.74	14.1	1.91	-3.100	2.58	-1.20	
40%-69%/>70%[a]	12.4	1.53	14.1	1.91	-1.700	2.45	-0.69	

Note. CSC = Central States Conference on the Teaching of Foreign Languages; NEC = Northeast Conference on the Teaching of Foreign Languages; PNCFL = Pacific Northwest Council for Languages; SCOLT = Southern Conference on Language Teaching; SWCOLT = Southwest Conference on Language Teaching.

[a]T-Test results for SES apply only to public schools where SES data are available.

Table D. Differences by School Level in the Percentage of Middle Schools and High Schools Offering Foreign Languages in 2008 and 1997

	2008		1997					
	x(1)	SE x(1)	x(2)	SE x(2)	x(1) - x(2)	Standard error of the difference	t	Significant ($p < .05$)
Middle w/combination in 2008	58.8	3.04	75.0	2.73	-16.200	4.09	-3.96	* (decrease)
High w/combination in 2008	91.1	1.69	90.0	1.55	1.100	2.29	0.48	
Middle w/out combination in 2008	58.3	3.02	75.0	2.73	-16.700	4.07	-4.10	* (decrease)
High w/out combination in 2008	94.7	2.13	90.0	2.73	4.700	3.46	1.36	

Note. The 1997 report included a separate category for combination schools. The first comparison includes combination schools in the 2008 data while the second comparison does not.

Table E. Differences by Metro Status, School Size, Region, and Socioeconomic Status in the Percentage of Middle Schools Offering Foreign Languages in 2008

	x(1)	SE x(1)	x(2)	SE x(2)	x(1) - x(2)	Standard error of the difference	t	Significant ($p < .05$)
Metro status								
Urban/Suburban	71.6	7.79	67.9	4.65	3.700	9.07	0.41	
Urban/Rural	71.6	7.79	44.3	4.93	27.300	9.22	2.96	*(difference)
Suburban/Rural	67.9	4.65	44.3	4.93	23.600	6.78	3.48	*(difference)
School size								
<400/400–999	29.2	7.41	68.3	3.76	-39.100	8.31	-4.71	*(difference)
<400/1,000–1,399	29.2	7.41	86.9	7.57	-57.700	10.59	-5.45	*(difference)
<400/>1,400	29.2	7.41	66.9	13.92	-37.700	15.77	-2.39	*(difference)
400-999/1,000–1,399	68.3	3.76	86.9	7.57	-18.600	8.45	-2.20	*(difference)
400-999/>1,400	68.3	3.76	66.9	13.92	1.400	14.42	0.10	
1,000–1,399/>1,400	86.9	7.57	66.9	13.92	20.000	15.85	1.26	
Region								
NEC/SCOLT	78.9	6.69	61.1	8.03	17.800	10.45	1.70	
NEC/SWCOLT	78.9	6.69	58.3	6.83	20.600	9.56	2.15	*(difference)
NEC/CSC	78.9	6.69	50.5	7.5	28.400	10.05	2.83	*(difference)
NEC/PNCFL	78.9	6.69	45.0	13.59	33.900	15.15	2.24	*(difference)
SCOLT/SWCOLT	61.1	8.03	58.3	6.83	2.800	10.54	0.27	
SCOLT/CSC	61.1	8.03	50.5	7.5	10.600	10.99	0.96	
SCOLT/PNCFL	61.1	8.03	45.0	13.59	16.100	15.79	1.02	
SWCOLT/CSC	58.3	6.83	50.5	7.5	7.800	10.14	0.77	
SWCOLT/PNCFL	58.3	6.83	45.0	13.59	13.300	15.21	0.87	
CSC/PNCFL	50.5	7.5	45.0	13.59	5.500	15.52	0.35	
Socioeconomic status								
<20%/20%–39%[a]	73.5	6.49	63.9	5.07	9.600	8.24	1.17	
<20%/40%–69%[a]	73.5	6.49	46.8	5.85	26.700	8.74	3.06	* (difference)
<20%/>70%[a]	73.5	6.49	45.3	12.39	28.200	13.99	2.02	* (difference)
20%–39%/40-69%[a]	63.9	5.07	46.8	5.85	17.100	7.74	2.21	* (difference)
20%–39%/>70%[a]	63.9	5.07	45.3	12.39	18.600	13.39	1.39	
40%–69%/>70%[a]	46.8	5.85	45.3	12.39	1.500	13.70	0.11	

Note. CSC = Central States Conference on the Teaching of Foreign Languages; NEC = Northeast Conference on the Teaching of Foreign Languages; PNCFL = Pacific Northwest Council for Languages; SCOLT = Southern Conference on Language Teaching; SWCOLT = Southwest Conference on Language Teaching.

[a]T-Test results for SES apply only to public schools where SES data are available.

Table F. Differences by Metro Status, School Size, Region, and Socioeconomic Status in the Percentage of High Schools Offering Foreign Languages in 2008

	x(1)	SE x(1)	x(2)	SE x(2)	x(1) - x(2)	Standard error of the difference	*t*	Significant (*p* < .05)
Metro status								
Urban/Suburban	87.6	4.19	96.2	1.09	-8.600	4.33	-1.99	*(difference)
Urban/Rural	87.6	4.19	89.8	2.64	-2.200	4.95	-0.44	
Suburban/Rural	96.2	1.09	89.8	2.64	6.400	2.86	2.24	*(difference)
School size								
<400/400–999	83.4	3.17	97.9	2.15	-14.500	3.83	-3.79	*(difference)
<400/1,000–1,399	83.4	3.17	100.0	0	-16.600	3.17	-5.24	*(difference)
<400/>1,400	83.4	3.17	100.0	0	-16.600	3.17	-5.24	*(difference)
400–999/1,000–1,399	97.9	2.15	100.0	0	-2.100	2.15	-0.98	
400–999/>1,400	97.9	2.15	100.0	0	-2.100	2.15	-0.98	
1,000–1,399/>1,400	100.0	0	100.0	0	0.000	0.00	0.00	
Region								
NEC/SCOLT	97.8	1.23	94.1	2.99	3.700	3.23	1.14	
NEC/SWCOLT	97.8	1.23	87.4	4.54	10.400	4.70	2.21	*(difference)
NEC/CSC	97.8	1.23	91.4	3.12	6.400	3.35	1.91	
NEC/PNCFL	97.8	1.23	74.5	11.08	23.300	11.15	2.09	*(difference)
SCOLT/SWCOLT	94.1	2.99	87.4	4.54	6.700	5.44	1.23	
SCOLT/CSC	94.1	2.99	91.4	3.12	2.700	4.32	0.62	
SCOLT/PNCFL	94.1	2.99	74.5	11.08	19.600	11.48	1.71	
SWCOLT/CSC	87.4	4.54	91.4	3.12	-4.000	5.51	-0.73	
SWCOLT/PNCFL	87.4	4.54	74.5	11.08	12.900	11.97	1.08	
CSC/PNCFL	91.4	3.12	74.5	11.08	16.900	11.51	1.47	
Socioeconomic status								
<20%/20%–39%[a]	94.2	4.07	100.0	0	-5.800	4.07	-1.43	
<20%/40%–69%[a]	94.2	4.07	92.1	4.32	2.100	5.94	0.35	
<20%/>70%[a]	94.2	4.07	75.1	12.78	19.100	13.41	1.42	
20%–39%/40%–69%[a]	100.0	0	92.1	4.32	7.900	4.32	1.83	
20%–39%/>70%[a]	100.0	0	75.1	12.78	24.900	12.78	1.95	
40%–69%/>70%[a]	92.1	4.32	75.1	12.78	17.000	13.49	1.26	

Note. CSC = Central States Conference on the Teaching of Foreign Languages; NEC = Northeast Conference on the Teaching of Foreign Languages; PNCFL = Pacific Northwest Council for Languages; SCOLT = Southern Conference on Language Teaching; SWCOLT = Southwest Conference on Language Teaching.

[a]T-Test results for SES apply only to public schools where SES data are available.

Table G. Differences by Metro Status, School Size, Region, and Socioeconomic Status in the Percentage of Secondary Schools Offering Foreign Languages in 2008

	x(1)	SE x(1)	x(2)	SE x(2)	x(1) - x(2)	Standard error of the difference	*t*	Significant ($p < .05$)
Metro status								
Urban/Suburban	81.9	3.47	83.9	2.5	-2.000	4.28	-0.47	
Urban/Rural	81.9	3.47	73.8	2.57	8.100	4.32	1.88	
Suburban/Rural	83.9	2.5	73.8	2.57	10.100	3.59	2.82	*(difference)
School size								
<400/400–999	69.7	3.32	80.3	2.61	-10.600	4.22	-2.51	*(difference)
<400/1,000–1,399	69.7	3.32	95.5	2.67	-25.800	4.26	-6.06	*(difference)
<400/>1,400	69.7	3.32	95.8	1.8	-26.100	3.78	-6.91	*(difference)
400–999/1,000–1,399	80.3	2.61	95.5	2.67	-15.200	3.73	-4.07	*(difference)
400–999/>1,400	80.3	2.61	95.8	1.8	-15.500	3.17	-4.89	*(difference)
1,000–1,399/>1,400	95.5	2.67	95.8	1.8	-0.300	3.22	-0.09	
Region								
NEC/SCOLT	90.7	2.69	82.4	3.56	8.300	4.46	1.86	
NEC/SWCOLT	90.7	2.69	75.8	4.23	14.900	5.01	2.97	*(difference)
NEC/CSC	90.7	2.69	76.7	3.25	14.000	4.22	3.32	*(difference)
NEC/PNCFL	90.7	2.69	60.6	8.22	30.100	8.65	3.48	*(difference)
SCOLT/SWCOLT	82.4	3.56	75.8	4.23	6.600	5.53	1.19	
SCOLT/CSC	82.4	3.56	76.7	3.25	5.700	4.82	1.18	
SCOLT/PNCFL	82.4	3.56	60.6	8.22	21.800	8.96	2.43	*(difference)
SWCOLT/CSC	75.8	4.23	76.7	3.25	-0.900	5.33	-0.17	
SWCOLT/PNCFL	75.8	4.23	60.6	8.22	15.200	9.24	1.64	
CSC/PNCFL	76.7	3.25	60.6	8.22	16.100	8.84	1.82	
Socioeconomic status								
<20%/20%–39%[a]	85.6	3.67	82.4	2.94	3.200	4.70	0.68	
<20%/40%–69%[a]	85.6	3.67	69.3	3.93	16.300	5.38	3.03	*(difference)
<20%/>70%[a]	85.6	3.67	60.2	8.91	25.400	9.64	2.64	*(difference)
20%–39%/40%–69%[a]	82.4	2.94	69.3	3.93	13.100	4.91	2.67	*(difference)
20%–39%/>70%[a]	82.4	2.94	60.2	8.91	22.200	9.38	2.37	*(difference)
40%–69%/>70%[a]	69.3	3.93	60.2	8.91	9.100	9.74	0.93	

Note. CSC = Central States Conference on the Teaching of Foreign Languages; NEC = Northeast Conference on the Teaching of Foreign Languages; PNCFL = Pacific Northwest Council for Languages; SCOLT = Southern Conference on Language Teaching; SWCOLT = Southwest Conference on Language Teaching.

[a]T-Test results for SES apply only to public schools where SES data are available.

Table H. Differences by Language and School Type in the Percentage of Elementary Schools Offering Spanish, French, Latin, Chinese, and German in 2008 and 1997

	2008		1997					
	x(1)	SE x(1)	x(2)	SE x(2)	x(1) - x(2)	Standard error of the difference	*t*	Significant ($p < .05$)
Total, Spanish	87.5	1.77	79.1	2.33	8.400	2.93	2.87	*(increase)
Public	81.5	2.75	80.3	3.02	1.200	4.08	0.29	
Private	91.8	1.98	77.4	3.65	14.400	4.15	3.47	*(increase)
Total, French	11.2	1.63	27.3	2.55	-16.100	3.03	-5.32	*(decrease)
Public	8.4	3.12	27.4	3.39	-19.000	4.61	-4.12	*(decrease)
Private	13.3	1.80	27.3	3.89	-14.000	4.29	-3.27	*(decrease)
Total, Latin	5.5	1.29	3.0	0.98	2.500	1.62	1.54	
Public	1.1	0.61	0.6	0.59	0.500	0.85	0.59	
Private	8.6	2.17	6.1	2.09	2.500	3.01	0.83	
Total, Chinese	3.3	0.77	0.3	0.31	3.000	0.83	3.61	*(increase)
Public	2.2	0.78	0.6	0.59	1.600	0.98	1.64	
Private[a]								
Total, German	2.1	0.62	4.5	1.19	-2.400	1.34	-1.79	
Public	0.7	0.7	6.5	1.87	-5.800	2.00	-2.90	*(decrease)
Private	3.0	1.00	1.6	1.09	1.400	1.48	0.95	

[a]Comparison not possible at the private school level due to no data for 1997.

Table I. Differences by Language and School Type in the Percentage of Secondary Schools Offering Spanish, French, Latin, Chinese, German, and Japanese in 2008 and 1997

	2008		1997					
	x(1)	SE x(1)	x(2)	SE x(2)	x(1) - x(2)	Standard error of the difference	*t*	Significant ($p < .05$)
Total, Spanish	93.2	1.42	93.2	0.78	0.000	1.62	0.00	
Public	94.4	1.68	92.2	0.89	2.200	1.90	1.16	
Private	89.1	2.39	99.8	0.38	-10.700	2.42	4.42	*(decrease)
Total, French	45.5	1.84	63.5	1.49	-18.000	2.37	7.60	*(decrease)
Public	48.5	2.24	62.4	1.61	-13.900	2.76	5.04	*(decrease)
Private	35.4	2.42	70.5	3.86	-35.100	4.56	7.70	*(decrease)
Total, German	14.3	1.23	24.0	1.32	-9.700	1.80	5.38	*(decrease)
Public	15.4	1.56	24.8	1.44	-9.400	2.12	4.43	*(decrease)
Private	10.6	1.60	19.4	3.35	-8.800	3.71	2.37	*(decrease)
Total, Latin	12.8	1.07	19.6	1.23	-6.800	1.63	4.17	*(decrease)
Public	8.5	1.15	16.3	1.23	-7.800	1.68	4.63	*(decrease)
Private	27.3	2.22	40.8	4.16	-13.500	4.72	2.86	*(decrease)
Total, Chinese	4.2	0.62	1.0	0.31	3.200	0.69	4.62	*(increase)
Public	3.5	0.71	1.1	0.35	2.400	0.79	3.03	*(increase)
Private	6.5	1.27	0.7	0.71	5.800	1.45	3.99	*(increase)
Total, Japanese	3.2	0.68	7.4	0.93	-4.200	1.15	3.64	*(decrease)
Public	3.2	0.78	6.9	0.97	-3.700	1.24	2.98	*(decrease)
Private	3.4	1.19	10.6	3.00	-7.200	3.22	2.23	*(decrease)

Table J. Differences by School Level in the Percentage of Secondary Schools Offering AP Language Classes in 2008 and 1997

	2008		1997					
	x(1)	SE x(1)	x(2)	SE x(2)	x(1) - x(2)	Standard error of the difference	*t*	Significant ($p < .05$)
All secondary schools	21.3	1.82	15.6	1.28	5.700	2.23	2.56	*(increase)
High schools only	40.8	3.78	15.6[a]	1.28	25.200	3.99	6.32	*(increase)

[a] This percentage represents all secondary schools. Percentage not available for high schools only in 1997.

Table K. Differences in the Percentage of Elementary Schools Using Various Types of Instructional Materials in 2008 and 1997

	2008	1997						
	x(1)	SE x(1)	x(2)	SE x(2)	x(1) - x(2)	Standard error of the difference	*t*	Significant ($p < .05$)
Textbooks	79.3	2.35	84.9	2.77	-5.600	3.64	-1.54	
Teacher-made	95.4	1.12	94.4	1.78	1.000	2.10	0.48	
Audio-visual	90.0	1.53	94.3	1.75	-4.300	2.32	-1.85	
Target culture literature	96.3	1.00	68.9	3.62	27.400	3.75	7.30	*(increase)
Authentic materials	81.1	2.06	74.2	3.42	6.900	3.99	1.73	
Internet	70.0	2.48	19.1	3.20	50.900	4.05	12.58	*(increase)
Computer-based	59.1	3.04	41.4	3.88	17.700	4.93	3.59	*(increase)
Technology	23.1	2.06	10.1	2.47	13.000	3.22	4.04	*(increase)
Other	37.4	5.7	16.5	4.67	20.900	7.37	2.84	*(increase)

Note. This comparison is between "yes" responses in 1997 and the sum of "frequently" and "sometimes" responses in 2008.

Table L. Differences in the Percentage of Secondary Schools Using Various Types of Instructional Materials in 2008 and 1997

	2008		1997					
	x(1)	SE x(1)	x(2)	SE x(2)	x(1) - x(2)	Standard error of the difference	*t*	Significant (*p* < .05)
Textbooks	2.3	1.06	2.1	0.51	0.200	1.18	0.17	
Teacher-made	2.5	0.91	4.7	0.78	-2.200	1.20	-1.84	
Audio-visual	2.7	1.05	1.0	0.35	1.700	1.11	1.54	
Target culture literature	1.7	0.75	16.8	1.42	-15.100	1.61	-9.40	*(decrease)
Authentic materials	7.5	1.62	7.7	0.98	-0.200	1.89	-0.11	
Internet	12.6	1.88	60.6	1.92	-48.000	2.69	-17.86	*(decrease)
Computer-based	20.0	2.55	48.3	1.91	-28.300	3.19	-8.88	*(decrease)
Technology	63.3	2.4	70.2	1.84	-6.900	3.02	-2.28	*(decrease)
Other	47.8	7.24	36.6	2.46	-38.800	7.65	-5.07	*(decrease)

Note. This comparison is between "no" responses in 1997 and "not at all" responses in 2008. A decrease in "no" responses means that the percentage of schools using the materials has increased.

Table M. Differences in the Amount of Target Language Used by Teachers in Secondary School Language Classes in 2008 and 1997

	2008		1997					
	x(1)	SE x(1)	x(2)	SE x(2)	x(1) - x(2)	Standard error of the difference	*t*	Significant (*p* < .05)
<50%	20.8	2.46	31.5	1.64	-10.700	2.96	-3.62	*(decrease)
50%–74%	43.5	2.73	46.6	1.76	-3.100	3.25	-0.95	
75%–100%	35.7	2.7	22.0	1.46	13.700	3.07	4.46	*(increase)

Note. Different categories were used in the 1997 and 2008 surveys for 75% and above. As a result, the comparison here is of combined responses in categories of 75% and above.

ABOUT THE AUTHORS

Nancy C. Rhodes is director of foreign language education at the Center for Applied Linguistics in Washington, D.C., where she is involved in language education research, test development, and foreign language teacher education. Her research interests focus on the teaching of foreign languages at the elementary school level, and her teaching experience includes English as a second language and Spanish. She and Ingrid Pufahl co-authored *Language by Video: An Overview of Foreign Language Instructional Videos for Children.* She is a founder and past executive secretary of the National Network for Early Language Learning. She has a B.A. in Latin American Area Studies from Denison University and an M.S. in sociolinguistics from Georgetown University.

Ingrid Pufahl is a research associate at the Center for Applied Linguistics in Washington, D.C. For the past 20 years, she has been involved in applied linguistic research, foreign language teaching, and teacher education. She has taught German and linguistics at the secondary school and university levels, both in the United States and in Germany. Her research interests include cross-cultural communication, second and foreign language education, and distance education. She is co-author of *Foreign Language Teaching: What the U.S. Can Learn From Other Countries,* with Nancy Rhodes and Donna Christian. She has an M.A.T. in German and physical education from the University of Hamburg, Germany, and a Ph.D. in sociolinguistics from Georgetown University.